WHAT THE
CEO WANTS YOU
TO KNOW

WHAT THE CEO WANTS YOU TO KNOW

YOU TO KNOW

HOW YOUR COMPANY
REALLY WORKS

RAM CHARAN

BUSINESS
BOOKS

1 3 5 7 9 10 8 6 4 2

Random House Business Books
20 Vauxhall Bridge Road
London SW1V 2SA

Random House Business Books is part of the Penguin Random House group of
companies whose addresses can be found at global.penguinrandomhouse.com.

Penguin
Random House
UK

This edition first published by Random House Business Books in 2017
First published in the United States by Crown Business in 2001

www.penguin.co.uk

A CIP catalogue record for this book is available from the British Library.

Hardback ISBN 9781847942166
Trade paperback ISBN 9781847942173

Printed and bound by Clays Ltd, St Ives plc

Penguin Random House is committed to a sustainable future for our business, our readers
and our planet. This book is made from Forest Stewardship Council® certified paper.

Dedicated to the hearts and souls of the joint family of twelve siblings and cousins living under one roof for fifty years, whose personal sacrifices made my formal education possible

CONTENTS

PART III

AN EDGE IN EXECUTION

PART IV

YOUR PERSONAL AGENDA

PART I

THE UNIVERSAL LANGUAGE OF BUSINESS

1

HOW THIS BOOK CAN HELP YOU

Think back to your school days and the best teacher you ever had. The one who seemed to know everything about his or her subject and had something all the other teachers lacked: the ability to boil down the complex ideas of the discipline—whether it was psychology, economics, mathematics, or chemistry—so that you really "got it."

Other teachers may have had a great depth of knowledge, or fancier credentials, but they couldn't turn on the lightbulb over your head. Instead of making something complex seem simple, they did the opposite—they made it harder to understand.

I've been in the business world for more than fifty years, beginning when I was a child in my family's small shoe store in India, then working as an engineer in Australia. From there, I moved to America, attended Harvard Business School, taught there and at Northwestern's Kellogg School of Management and Boston University, and have been advising CEOs and serving on boards of directors at companies large and small around the world ever since. The one thing I've noticed in all that time is that the best CEOs are like the best teachers. They are able to take the complexity and mystery out of business by focusing on the moneymaking fundamentals. And they make sure that everyone in the company, not just their executive colleagues, understands those building blocks of business.

You could say that in doing so they have their self-interest at heart, since the company is more successful when everyone knows how the business works. But it's not just the CEO who benefits. People feel more connected to their work and have greater job satisfaction when they really understand how their organization works. And as the company grows profitably year after year there are greater opportunities for them to expand their careers and make more money, and the company can make a greater contribution to the community. The same applies to a nonprofit or government agency. (See the box "Wait! This Is True of Nonprofits, NGOs, and Government Agencies, Too?") That's why the best CEOs everywhere work so hard to explain things. And that's why I want to share with you, in the words of the book's title, what the CEO wants you to know, so that you can learn, grow, and make a greater contribution to not only your organization but the world around you.

This Is Far Easier Than You Think

It turns out that business is very simple and very logical. There are universal principles that apply whether you sell fruit from a stand or run a Fortune 500 company. Every organization must serve its customers, manage its cash effectively, use its assets wisely, and constantly improve and grow.

These are the basics. This is business boiled down to its

essentials. And those essentials are present in every company anywhere on the globe, despite differences of cultures, dialects, or government regulations. It's always been this way. Think once more about your school days. Once you understood that the atom was made up of protons, electrons, and neutrons, you had the fundamentals to help you solve any chemistry problem.

WAIT! THIS IS TRUE OF NONPROFITS, NGOS, AND GOVERNMENT AGENCIES, TOO?

Sometimes people are surprised when I say that *everyone* needs to understand the fundamentals of business. They say they work for a government agency, NGO (nongovernmental organization), or nonprofit (such as a charity or volunteer group), and this discussion can't possibly apply to them.

But it does, although some of the terminology is different.

Let's take just one of the four key essentials of any organization—managing cash effectively. True, NGOs and government entities usually don't sell things to generate cash, but still they must make sure they have enough money to operate both today and in the future. For a nonprofit, that money usually comes from donations; government agencies receive funding.

Similarly, just as in for-profit businesses, NGOs and government agencies need to manage their cash well. Otherwise they will cease to exist, in the case of a charity, or be reorganized or shut down, in the case of a government agency.

The takeaway is simple: all of us, no matter what we do for a living, will be better at our jobs if we learn how moneymaking tools are applied within our organizations.

I want to show you that it's the same with business. When you know the fundamentals, you "get" the basics for how *any* business operates.

My goal in writing this book is to give you the benefit of my experiences observing how some of the most successful people in business think and act. You will see what they do to make their companies—and their people—world-class.

WHEN I WROTE THAT THIS IS WHAT THE CEO WANTS YOU TO KNOW, I MEANT IT

You might be interested in the origins of the book.

Jacques Nasser, then the CEO of Ford, wanted his employees to know more than what it took to do their jobs well. He also wanted them to understand the entire business so that they could see where their contributions fit in and how they could help the whole company, not just their particular department.

He asked me to teach a course to a couple of hundred managers. On day three he sat in at the back of the room, and when we took a break he said: "This is exactly what I want, but it is going to take too long to have you teach everyone. I want you to write a simple, clear book capturing everything you are going to talk about."

And so I did.

The best CEOs and street vendors think the same way. They know their cash situation. They know which are their most profitable items. They understand the importance of keeping their products moving off the shelves, and they know their customers because satisfying customers is what ultimately keeps you in business.

What your CEO wants you to know is how these fundamentals of business work—*and work together*—in your organization. By investing a couple of hours in this book, you will. Once you understand them, there is no limit on where you can go in your organization.

Before We Begin

While I wrote this book for everyone who wants and needs a greater understanding of how their organization really works, there are two groups I will be singling out for particular attention.

The first is *millennials,* those 83 million of you born between 1982 and 2000, the largest cohort who has ever lived. (You outnumber your baby boomer parents by more than 7 million.) Millennials are the drivers of the digital revolution and are now firmly ensconced in the workforce. Those of you who truly understand how your business works will soon be assuming top leadership positions in your organizations.

> **Business is always changing, but the basics remain the same.**

The second is the *business-to-business (B2B) salesforce.* The reason for that is simple. There is an ongoing trend that is only going to accelerate. Rob Bernshteyn, CEO of Coupa— the cloud-based "spend management" software firm—calls it value-as-a-service. It's the simple idea that every organization must deliver to the customer something that will lead to quantifiable improvement: this much in cost reductions, this much improvement in lead generation, this much of a rise in revenue, this much of an increase in employee retention, and the like.

In the coming years, every corporate purchaser will say, "You want me to buy what you are selling? Fine. Here are the very specific, quantifiable outcomes I want. Prove to me that you are going to deliver them and I'll buy. If you can't, I won't."

If you are selling or providing services to people who have this attitude, you have to understand your business and theirs in order to make the sale.

How This Book Is Organized

Let me tell you what you will see in the pages ahead.

In the first half of the book we will explain the building blocks of every business—cash, inventory turns, profitable growth, and satisfying customers—and see how all CEOs, whether they run start-ups, online companies, or large traditional ones, use each one.

Once you understand the tools, we will show you how to apply them. So in Part II we will be talking about how business gets done today.

I said "today" for a reason. When I started, business was hierarchical. Information passed up and down through a formal chain of command, and there were sign-offs and approvals at every step. Today, though, two of the key skills you need are collaboration and integration. Collaboration is necessary because more and more work is being done in teams, as organizations of

every type realize that people at the top are not the sole deposi-
tary of all knowledge. That collaboration, of course, is taking
place outside the company as well as inside, as organizations
work with vendors, suppliers, and even customers to create new
products and services.

> **Today, you have to be not only a team player, in the truest sense of the word, but you have to be an integrator as well.**

And we will be talking about integration because increasingly that work cuts across all functions. You need to have everyone work together seamlessly in a way that creates speed,
decisiveness, and value for customers, employees, and shareholders.

Think for a moment about the creation of the Amazon
Echo, the voice-controlled device that can generate to-do lists,
play music, set alarms, provide news and weather updates in
real time, and control the smart devices in your home. It took
people who knew speech recognition software, artificial intelligence, and electronics (among other skills) sharing expertise
and making trade-offs and adjustments to make the product a
reality. And it had to happen quickly to beat the competition to
the market.

Those people understood the building blocks of the business. For example, everything about Echo was created with the
customer—one of our business fundamentals—in mind. The
team that created Echo knew the device had to execute every
request in literally a second or less, or the consumer would be
frustrated. So that became a non-negotiable objective.

From there, we will discuss how you can get things done. Working together and integration are all well and good, but you still need to accomplish things. You need to execute. We will show you how.

And finally we will talk about your part in the big picture of how your organization works and what you can do to make sure both you and the people who employ you thrive.

With that by way of background, let's begin.

2

WHAT THE BEST CEOS AND STREET VENDORS SHARE: THE ESSENCE OF BUSINESS THINKING

The language of business is the same everywhere.

It's 11:00 a.m. on a workday in midtown Manhattan. To be exact, you're at the corner of 48th Street and Sixth Avenue. (Only people who have never been here before call it Avenue of the Americas.) The buildings that make up Rockefeller Center surround you.

If you used your smartphone to call up an overhead shot from Google Maps, you would see you are a short walk from all the landmarks they show in the movies every time they want to establish that what is going on is taking place in New York City. Most of the theater district is to the west, and so are Times Square and the Port Authority Bus Terminal. The Museum of Modern Art is slightly north and a bit east, and almost due east is St. Patrick's Cathedral—it is basically on the other side of the Rockefeller Center skating rink, which has the huge Christmas tree, complete with thousands of lights, in front of it every December.

From where you are you can basically throw the proverbial stone and hit countless media companies—*Bloomberg Businessweek* is in the building behind you, and Fox News is directly across the street with its electronic ticker running headlines twenty-four hours a day on a marquee outside. The publisher of this book is less than a ten-minute walk away on Broadway.

But what is most interesting is the number of one-person retailers—and that is what they are, CEOs of one-person companies—that line the sidewalk. There are hot dog carts on either side of the street. You're standing next to a small food truck called Rockefeller Halal Foods, and adjacent to it is a woman selling sunglasses and scarves. Next to her is a woman who will sketch your portrait for $5.

It is even more crowded as you look up the block to 49th and Sixth. There are fifteen different food carts selling everything from coffee and Danish to Korean barbeque to Indian curry. And between here and there you'll find a person selling secondhand paperbacks and another offering imitation designer purses.

Even if you have never been to Manhattan, you have probably encountered a similar scene where people were selling goods from tables and carts right there on the street. Anywhere you go in the world, you can find street vendors hawking their wares: Chicago, Mexico City, São Paulo, Mumbai, Barcelona, San Francisco, Tokyo, Seoul, Shanghai.

If you bought something from them, you probably made your purchase quickly and went on your way. I bet it never occurred to you to think about their business. But if you do, you will notice something surprising. No matter where in the world they are or what they sell, they talk about—and think about—

their business in remarkably similar ways. They speak a universal language of business.

Perhaps even more surprising is that the street vendor's language is the same as the language of Tim Cook (he's the CEO
of Apple), Mark Fields (CEO of Ford), Ginni Rometty (CEO of
IBM), and Marillyn Hewson (CEO of Lockheed Martin). It's
the same as Akio Toyoda's (Toyota's president), Tadashi Yanai's
(CEO of the global retailer Uniqlo), and Rahul Bhatia's (CEO of
IndiGo, the low-cost Indian airline).

> **When it comes to running a business, street vendors and the CEOs of the world's largest and most successful companies think exactly the same way. The complexities of their businesses are different; their approach is not.**

You can hear it for yourself. The CEOs of publicly held
companies frequently—usually quarterly—hold conference
calls with stock analysts (we will talk about them later). You can
listen in on those calls; the company's website will provide a
dial-in number. If you do, you will hear the CEOs talking about
sales, margins, profitable growth, customers, and the like.

There are differences, of course, between running a huge
corporation and a small shop, and we'll get to those, but the
basics are the same.

The people who run huge, global organizations are often
referred to as managers or leaders, but the best ones think of
themselves as businesspeople first. I know because I've been
permitted to observe some of these business leaders, and others

like them, firsthand. For more than five decades I have had the privilege of working one-on-one with some of the world's most successful business leaders, including Jack Welch and Jeff Immelt of GE, Brian Moynihan of Bank of America, Andrea Jung of Avon, Robert Bradway of Amgen, and A. G. Lafley of Procter & Gamble. I've seen the way their minds work, the way they cut through the largest and most complex issues to the fundamentals of business.

I learned those fundamentals as a child growing up in a small agricultural town in northern India. There I watched my older brothers struggle together to make a living selling shoes from their small shop. With no experience and no formal training, they competed head-to-head against others in the town who were also trying to eke out a living. They learned, and over time built a name brand and earned the trust of the local farmers who were their customers. Other shops have come and gone, but ours has flourished, and my nephews continue to run it to this day, nearly sixty-five years after my brothers opened its doors.

That shoe shop paid for my education and allowed me to venture far beyond my roots. At age nineteen, with an engineering degree in hand, I took a job at a gas utility company in Sydney, Australia. The CEO discovered I had a nose for business, and I soon found myself working on pricing strategies and investment analyses instead of designing pipeline networks. My interest in business proved to be irrepressible, and that CEO encouraged me to go to Harvard Business School, where I earned an MBA, then a doctorate, and later taught for six years. Since then I have had the opportunity to advise hundreds of CEOs in the United States, India, Brazil, Japan, Australia, and Europe and to teach business to tens of thousands more.

In my early days of consulting—as I worked with businesses of different sizes, in different industries, and in different cultures—I was struck by the similarities among successful business leaders. I saw that regardless of the size or type of business, a good CEO had a way of bringing the most complex business down to the fundamentals—the same fundamentals I learned in the family shoe store.

> **Anyone who figures out a clear way to make money has business acumen, or what some people call street smarts.**

They never lose sight of the basics. Their intense focus on them is, in fact, the secret to their success. Like the street vendor, they have a keen sense of how a business makes money. *And all of us need to learn how moneymaking tools are applied.*

Remember Your Roots

Many successful CEOs have had experiences early in their lives similar to that of a street vendor, giving root to their business thinking.

Leslie H. Wexner grew up working in his parents' small women's clothing store in Columbus, Ohio. Think of the challenges faced by small, independent retailers like Wexner's parents. They have to decide what customers to try to attract and how to draw them in; what merchandise to offer; where to buy it and how much to buy and at what cost. Then they must figure what to charge and how to design and arrange their store. They have to put in long, long hours because every decision matters.

His parents' small store is where Les Wexner learned the universal language of business and first tested his business thinking. In studying his parents' accounting ledgers while they took a rare vacation, he realized that only a few of the items they offered were profitable. He kept that thought in mind when he eventually opened a women's store of his own in Columbus, one he called the Limited because he only stocked profitable items. He still thinks the same way even as the Limited has become L Brands, a $13 billion retailer that earns more than $2 billion a year from its Victoria's Secret, Pink, Bath & Body Works, La Senze, and Henri Bendel stores.

Growing up in a small business, you can't help but absorb the fundamentals.

How About You?

You may not have grown up in your family's business. And chances are you've built your career in one area of your company, such as sales, finance, or production. These specializations, usually known as business functions, are sometimes also called chimneys or silos. That's because most people take their first job at a corporation in one business function and move up within that function as they get promoted. Thus, it appears as if they're moving vertically through a chimney or silo.

Those career tracks tend to narrow your perspective and influence the decisions and trade-offs you make every day. What's best or most exciting for your department is not necessarily best for the company as a whole. If you are an engineer, you might be tempted to make a product loaded with features, but the company may not be able to charge enough for it given the competition, and so will lose money on every sale. That's why in its early days, Hewlett-Packard demanded that its engineers create superior products that could demand superior margins. They made sure the engineers took into account the customer and the competition as well as HP's technology capabilities.

The point is simple: you may be a top-notch professional, good at marketing or IT, but are you really a businessperson? Regardless of your job or silo, you need to develop your understanding of how the total organization makes money.

As you learn to see your company as a whole and make decisions that enhance its overall performance, you will help make meetings less bureaucratic and more focused on the business issues. Time will pass quickly, as it does when discussions are constructive and energizing. You'll get more excited about your job because you'll see that your suggestions and decisions are helping the business grow and prosper.

Learning to speak the universal language of business will advance your career.

When you learn to speak the universal language of business, you'll tear down the walls that separate you, a functional chimney/silo person, from the senior executives who speak a language you may not understand today. You'll feel more connected to your company and your work. And the range of opportunities open to you will expand.

The Street Vendor's Skill

How does a street vendor hawking fruit in a small Indian town make a living? Someone with a $250,000 undergraduate education and an MBA might say that he "anticipates demand." But our street vendor doesn't know the buzzwords. He doesn't own a computer. He just has his understanding of business fundamentals. He has to determine what to buy that morning—what quantity, what quality, and what assortment—based on what he thinks he can sell that day (his sales forecast).

Then he has to figure out what prices to charge and be nimble enough to adjust them as needed during the day. He doesn't want to carry the fruit (the inventory) home with him. If it begins to decay, it will be of less value tomorrow. Another reason he doesn't want anything left over is that he needs the cash.

All day long he has to weigh whether to cut prices, when to cut them, and by how much. If he is indecisive or makes a wrong trade-off, he may lose out. If he cuts the price too early, he may not make a profit for the day. If he waits too long, he could be left with rotting inventory.

It is no different in companies. Say the Federal Reserve increases interest rates. Demand for automobiles might suddenly drop, because people cannot afford the resulting higher rates on car loans, and the automotive companies may not be able to adjust their production levels quickly enough. If that is the case, they will end up with excess inventory. The companies then have to scramble to get rid of it to collect cash. That's when you start seeing TV commercials telling you that one of the car companies is offering rebates (or maybe all of them are). Both rebates and increased spending on advertising hurt profits.

Also, such selling approaches can begin to cheapen the image of the brand. Yet companies sometimes endure those negatives because they need the cash.

Back to Our Street Vendor

Let's take a closer look at our street vendor's day-to-day operations.

Each morning when the street vendor sets up his cart, he puts the best-looking fruit in front (retailers call this display). He watches the competition—what they're selling and for how much (market analysis). And the whole time, he's thinking about not just today but also tomorrow. If he has trouble selling his produce, he might have to cut the price (increase the value to the customer), rearrange the display, or yell louder (advertise) to attract attention to his stand. Maybe tomorrow he'll find a better price at which to buy, or change the assortment of fruits and vegetables (the product mix). If something doesn't work, he adjusts. He is doing all this in his head.

How does he know if he's doing well? If he has money left over at the end of the day. Everyone understands cash, money in the pocket. Every language has a word for this. The street vendor constantly thinks about cash: Does he have enough cash? How can he get more cash? Will he continue to be able to generate cash?

What happens to the street vendor who doesn't have cash at the end of the day? It causes misery all over. He loses face. The tension in the family is almost unbearable. And yes, it's true, in India his family may not have enough to eat. Such consequences focus the mind.

And whether the street vendor realizes it or not, his sub-conscious is pondering something even deeper: how will he buy goods for the next day? He needs cash to stay in business.

So do companies. You hear all the time about companies that are strapped for cash. Maybe they produced too many things that didn't sell and the cash got tied up in inventory. Or they invested money in a plant that's too big and the company can't generate enough money from it. Or the company sold its products on credit to distributors or retailers and got paid late or not at all.

When companies can't generate enough cash, they often borrow it, increasing their costs, since they have to pay inter-est on the loans. If they borrow heavily and don't correct the problem that created the cash shortage, they will have trouble repaying the loans. Some end up bankrupt because they lost sight of this business fundamental.

Back to the street vendor. How vendors buy fruit varies from country to country. In India, when personal cash savings are hard to accumulate, the vendor may have to borrow cash to buy the fruit he plans to sell. To make a living, he has to make enough money to pay back what he borrowed, with some left over.

Every time he sells a melon, for example, he makes just a lit-tle bit of money. His profit, the difference between what he pays for the fruit and what he sells it for, is low. His profit margin—the cash he gets to keep as a percentage of the total cash he takes in—is around 5 percent. (Different companies have different terminology for this basic idea. Some call it return on sales, or operating margin. You need to know what your company calls it. But what's really important is the idea, which I'll explain more fully later.)

Let's say our street vendor borrows 4,000 rupees (Rs. 4,000 is about $60). That is his capital, the money available to him to run his business. He uses it as a deposit on Rs. 40,000 worth of fruit. The fruit is his only asset. If he sells all Rs. 40,000 worth of fruit at a 2 percent profit margin (after deducting all expenses), he will make a profit of Rs. 800. In other words, he used his Rs. 4,000 in capital to make Rs. 800, so his "return on invested capital" is 20 percent. (We will talk more about these calculations in Chapter 3.)

Can the street vendor raise his prices to make more profit? Only so much. If his price is too high, his customers will go to another vendor. Can he find a way to pay less for the fruit? Maybe. But if he buys fruit that's overripe, his customers will know the difference. Maybe some kinds of fruit are more profitable than others. Should he sell only the most profitable ones?

In the automotive business in the early 1990s, Ford gained a decisive financial advantage over General Motors by changing its product mix. Ford was quick to recognize the increasing desire for sport utility vehicles and light trucks. While continuing to offer a full range of vehicles, Ford shifted some of its production from cars to SUVs and trucks, which are more profitable. It won the leading market share in North America in these product areas, despite the fact that GM was bigger.

This kind of thinking happens all the time. Recall the introduction of the iPhone. Yes, it was a revolutionary product (there was no keyboard!) that in essence was a new kind of personal computer, one you could hold in your hand. But what people forget is what Apple did at the very beginning, with the phone's introduction.

Up until that point, every time a company such as Black-Berry or Nokia introduced a new phone, they offered it to every cell service provider. Invariably, the providers would sell the phone cheaply, as an inducement to get people to sign up for their service.

That's a classic business strategy. But the problem with it, from the perspective of the companies that make the phones, is that it squeezed what they could charge the cell service providers. If Verizon, Sprint, and T-Mobile were going to sell the phones cheaply, they weren't willing to pay a lot for them. In essence, the phone companies, not the manufacturers, were controlling the price of the phones.

Apple took a different route. Instead of offering the iPhone to every carrier, it initially created a five-year exclusive with AT&T. The arrangement allowed Apple to charge far more for the revolutionary phone. Businesspeople, just like the street vendor, have to think creatively like this all the time.

The street vendor has many realities to deal with. If he makes the wrong judgment repeatedly, he will find it hard to make a living. If he doesn't give his customers a fair deal, they will not return and he will develop a bad reputation, decreasing sales even further. If, on the other hand, he gives people a good deal every time while making a profit, he builds their trust and loyalty to his brand.

The upshot: he has to be customer focused.

Learning from the Street Vendor

Running a one-person business such as a fruit cart may seem simple, but it requires many decisions. These judgments are made intuitively—without the benefit of banks of computers, sophisticated forecasting techniques, or off-site meetings at expensive resorts. The skill and business acumen of the street vendor is passed down from generation to generation in cities and villages around the world. Children listen to their elders and observe them at work, just as I did, and participate in the business by working there part-time. They intuitively come to understand how a business operates.

My experience growing up is typical. I still recall how every evening at around nine o'clock I would follow my brothers home from their shop and we'd gather on the rooftop to escape the sweltering heat inside the house. We discussed the day's events—which customers came or didn't come, what sold or didn't, whom we needed to collect money from the next morning, and what the two most prosperous shops in the village were doing (best practices).

I saw my older brothers—I was the youngest—struggle every day to build relationships with customers (we would call it building their brand) and make the right adjustments in the mix and prices of the shoes they sold. Every time they made a sale, a competitor—whose shop shared a common wall with ours—tried to persuade the customer to return the shoes to us and buy from him. It was hand-to-hand combat. Yet at the end of the day, our family made ends meet. Although we didn't use fancy terminology, we were learning the basics of making money and creating value for "shareholders" (in this case, our family members).

You, too, can hone your business acumen by mastering the basics of moneymaking: customers, cash generation, return on invested capital, and growth.

3

EVERY BUSINESS IS THE SAME INSIDE: THE FOUR THINGS EVERY COMPANY EVERYWHERE NEEDS TO MASTER

In every business, the basic building blocks are always the same.

Moneymaking in business has four parts: satisfying customer needs better than the competition, generating cash, producing a sufficient return on the money invested in the business (your capital), and growing profitably. Most people know how to do one or two of those things really well. True businesspeople understand all four parts individually *as well as the relationships between them.* By the time we are done with this chapter you will, too.

> **Businesspeople have an insatiable desire to cut through to the fundamental building blocks of moneymaking.**

Customers, cash generation, return on invested capital, and growth. Everything about a business flows from this nucleus.

Is the business attracting and retaining customers? Does the business generate cash and earn a good return on the money invested in the business? Is it growing? If the answer to those questions is yes, common sense tells you that the business is doing well. If this four-part core is not right, the company will eventually falter.

HOW THE RELATIONSHIP WORKS

We said true businesspeople understand not only the building blocks of business but also how satisfying customer needs, generating cash, producing a sufficient return on invested capital, and growing profitably work together. Here's an everyday example.

A company plans to introduce a new product. It obviously hopes it will sell well at a good price so that the company can grow profitably and produce a sufficient return. To do that, the head of marketing wants to create a big advertising campaign to generate interest and hopefully boost sales, and the head of manufacturing wants to build up inventory to meet anticipated demand.

But both those things—spending big on an ad campaign and building more product—consume cash. So, growing sales on the one hand and using cash for ad campaigns and inventory building on the other must be balanced.

Should the product not be right for the market, the company will have to cut prices—perhaps below cost—to convert that excess inventory into cash, and the advertising campaign will have been a waste of money.

Don't let the lack of a business school education or the size of your company obscure the simplicity of your business. Cut through to the nucleus. If your business shows deterioration in one or more of the four core areas, use common sense to fix it. If you do, you are on your way to thinking and acting like a true businessperson and a potential CEO.

Let's go through each of the four parts individually. We will connect all four later in this chapter.

Customers

It all starts here. If you don't have a customer, you don't have a business. You must fill a need or fix a problem customers have. The street vendor knows his customers well. Simply by watching them, he can detect whether they like his fruit or whether their preferences are changing. CEOs who truly understand how their business works—the ones who have street smarts— have the same close connection with their customers and know their company cannot exist without satisfying them. That belief is universal.

Although many companies today use analytics to parse every customer interaction, and constantly do surveys and focus groups to try to understand customer behaviors and needs, the best CEOs don't rely on clinical data alone. Seeing is indeed believing. That's why CEOs like Indra Nooyi of PepsiCo, A. G. Lafley of Procter & Gamble, and Tim Cook of Apple make a point of visiting stores to make their own personal observations.

You need to do this, too. Everyone has access to the same consumer data, reads the same trade papers, and attends the same industry conferences. If you merely behave as your competition does, you will never outperform them. That's why you want to observe all the interactions with your product from initial awareness of the product to its purchase and usage—the end-to-end customer experience. You want to talk to the distributors and wholesalers (if your company has them) as well as the end users to really understand what is going on.

SEEING FOR YOURSELF

One of the best retailers I know spends just about every Saturday at one of his stores around the country. He wants to see for himself what shopping bags from other retailers customers are carrying; he wants to know which stores they visit after they leave his; and, equally important, he wants to see how many people leave his store empty-handed after considering the merchandise.

On each visit, he makes it a point to talk to at least ten customers—he identifies himself not as the CEO, but just as someone who works for the company—to hear from people firsthand. He gets information and insights that all the numbers in the world won't show. He gets to understand how his customers are thinking. He isn't trying to sell them anything. He is there to learn.

CEOs like this know that if they become removed from the action, they may miss important changes and opportunities in the marketplace. And that can be devastating, since the customer is ultimately responsible for their organization's success.

If you have an insight, test it with consumers to see if you are right. Similarly, spend time studying where you think your industry might be going, and how the consumer's taste or lifestyle is changing. And once you think you know, talk to customers for confirmation. Firsthand information is always best.

At your company, you may talk about the people who buy your products as "customers." But they may not be the people who ultimately use the product—the "consumers." It's important to understand both. When P&G develops new products, it tries to understand the needs and wants of the *consumer*, but many of its processes—logistics, discounts, merchandising— are geared to serve *customers* such as Target.

As you think about both consumers and customers, keep it simple and specific. What are consumers buying? It might not be the physical product alone. Maybe they're buying reliability, trustworthiness, convenience, service, or the entire customer experience, whether in the store or online.

> ## Do you know what your customers are really buying from you and why?

When you can't get the prices and margins you used to, talk to consumers to understand why. Deal with them directly, unfiltered, not through distributors or other middlemen. No matter what your job, develop your skill in observing customers. If Nokia and BlackBerry had done that immediately after the iPhone was launched, they might not have miscalculated the devastating impact Apple would have on their business.

People talk about customer loyalty. But you have to earn that loyalty every time you come in contact with the customer. Customers need a simple reason to buy from you. You have to give them something they really need. It could be a low price. But it is equally possible that it is quality, service, or the solution to a problem they have. You can find out what they need—from them. That's common sense. But you would be surprised how often this business common sense is lacking.

Make sure you can never be accused of that. The CEO wants you to know your company's customers.

Cash Generation

Cash generation is one of several important indications of your company's moneymaking ability.

> **Don't lose sight of cash generation— the difference between all the cash that flows into the business and all the cash that flows out in a given time period.**

An astute businessperson wants to know: Does the business generate enough cash? What are the sources of its cash generation? How is the cash being used? Businesspeople who fail to ask these questions and/or don't figure out the answers eventually stumble.

Cash generation is the difference between all the cash that flows into the business and all the cash that flows out in a given time period. You may have heard it described as "cash flow," which is a shorthand version of the idea. I prefer to use "cash generation" because it forces everyone to understand both parts of the concept: the money that flows in, and the money that flows out.

Cash flows into the corporation in the form of cash, checks, and credit cards for the sale of its products. Cash flows out for things such as salaries, taxes, and payments to suppliers.

The street vendor conducts all his business in cash. His customers pay him in cash, and he pays his supplier in cash the same day. For him, cash and income are one and the same.

But most companies extend credit, so cash and income are different. They make a sale and add it to their income now but collect the money later. Similarly, they buy something now and pay for it later. They have accounts receivable (money customers owe them) and accounts payable (money they owe their suppliers). The timing of these payments affects cash generation.

Cash generation can be a problem for even the largest companies for any number of reasons: margins are too low, expenses are too high, or it takes too long to collect receivables, for example. The automobile industry has a history of having problems with cash generation. Chrysler ran out of cash in the early 1980s; Volkswagen did, too, in the late 1980s. And the classic example is probably GM, which was forced to file for bankruptcy in 2009. When you don't have enough cash and you can't borrow, you go bankrupt.

But it is not just big manufacturing firms that get in trouble. One of the clearest examples of problems with cash generation was in, would you believe, a management consulting firm. The senior partners had borrowed heavily to buy the company and therefore needed a lot of cash every month to make the interest payments. At one point it became clear that they were running out of cash. The only solution, it seemed, was to sell a piece of the business, which of course would diminish each partner's ownership stake.

Then, just before the deal was struck, the CEO had an insight that saved the partners' share of the business. She realized that clients were delaying payment. Accounts receivable—money clients owed the firm—was ninety days (meaning it took ninety days, on average, from the time the firm sent out an invoice until the time it got paid) instead of the forty-five-day industry average.

She took charge and assigned the CFO to put a system in place to speed up collections. She also got the partners to send invoices as projects progressed instead of waiting for the end of the month. Those simple changes improved cash flow and allowed the business to keep running.

> **Running out of cash is a common problem for start-ups in Silicon Valley and elsewhere. It takes longer to get the product into the marketplace than expected, or the costs of getting under way are substantially higher than budgeted.**

Cash gives you the ability to stay in business. It is a company's oxygen supply. Lack of cash, a decrease in cash, or increased consumption of cash spells trouble, even if the other elements of moneymaking—such as profit margin and growth—look good.

Every company is required to show in its annual report

where the cash came from and went during the year. Do you know whether your company is a net cash generator? And why it is, or isn't? If it is not generating cash, is it because your management is investing to grow the company, or because you have too much inventory, or expenses are too high, or it's taking too long to collect receivables, or the company has borrowed too heavily and is struggling to make payments?

If you work for a large company, does your division generate cash? Sometimes you hear a division president say, "I'm managing my division for cash, not growth." In that case, top management might have decided, for example, to use the cash from one division serving a slow-growth market to fund the research and development (R&D), marketing, or plant expansion of another division in a fast-growth sector.

Or sometimes a company is owned by family members who depend on the business as their main source of income. Such companies are often "managed for cash," meaning the family expects the business to generate money—which is paid to them in the form of dividends—to meet their immediate needs.

Everybody Counts

Most people can understand cash on a small, maybe personal scale. For example, if your bills are due before your paycheck arrives, what happens?

In a large company, however, some people lose sight of cash. Many think that it is the sole responsibility of the finance department.

> **No matter what kind of organization you work for—a for-profit company, a nonprofit, or a government agency— understanding where the cash comes from and where it goes is important. All people in an organization, not just those in finance, need to know how their job affects cash generation (or consumption) if their career is going to thrive.**

But everyone in a company must be aware that his or her actions use cash or generate cash. A sales rep who negotiates a thirty-day payment from a customer instead of forty-five days is cash wise. The company gets the money sooner and frees up cash—that is, the cash is available to use for other things. A plant manager whose poor scheduling results in accumulation of a lot of inventory consumes cash, because the company won't be able to free up that cash until the inventory is sold.

Even mailroom clerks have a role to play in cash generation. They sort and deliver the mail—letters, bills, and checks. Suppose Friday morning's mail is not sorted and delivered until that afternoon. Maybe the checks don't get to the right department until 4:30 p.m. By then, the people in accounts receivable are getting ready to go home. They decide they'll open the mail on Monday. When does the check turn into cash? Three days after it arrives.

Also think about when the mail gets sent. In many companies, invoices prepared after 2:00 p.m. on Friday aren't sent out until Monday morning, simply because that is the way it has always been done and nobody is paying attention to cash generation. By getting the invoices sent out before the end of the day Friday, the company could receive payments two days sooner, improving its cash situation.

So lots of people can keep the cash flowing, including the people in the mailroom. You need to know your company's cash situation—and what you can do to help it.

A CAUTIONARY TALE

Perhaps the best recent example of the importance of cash management is what happened to Webvan, one of the great dot-com failures.

On the surface, Webvan seemed like a great idea. Customers would order their groceries online and have them delivered right to their door.

In writing about Webvan, Peter Relan, who was the company's head of technology, said the marketing strategy was simple: Webvan would offer the quality and selection of the upscale chain Whole Foods at traditional supermarket prices.

While that certainly was appealing, it meant the company would have lower margins than an upscale retailer. To get around that problem, Webvan would be heavily automated, using state-of-the-art warehouses it would design and build to make fulfilling orders as efficient as possible.

This could have worked, but the company simply expanded too fast. The initial plan was to open in twenty-six metropolitan areas, each being served by one of the company's warehouses, which cost about $35 million each. That meant the warehouses alone cost more than $900 million. Add to those payments the cost of the expensive computer systems needed to run the operation, salaries for the company's 3,500 employees, and all the specialized delivery vans, and the company was going through $125 million a quarter. Profits didn't materialize soon enough, so cash flowed out much faster than it flowed in.

About four years after it began, the company simply ran out of cash and went out of business.

In recent years, some very smart businesspeople have figured out highly efficient ways to generate cash. Many of these efforts focus on inventory, which ties up cash. Look at Amazon, one of the pioneers of Internet retailing. When Amazon first started and just sold books, it did not carry inventory. That gave it a huge cash advantage over traditional booksellers, which had lots of books in lots of bookstores and warehouses. Amazon would receive book orders online and ship them from someone else's distribution facility to the customer. Amazon got paid by the customer's credit card company when the books were shipped, but it didn't pay for the books until many weeks later. It generated cash and used it for marketing, resulting in more sales.

Amazon remains partly committed to this kind of approach. Some 40 percent of the items sold by the company in 2015, according to the *Wall Street Journal*, were provided by third-party merchants who list their products on the Amazon website but handle fulfillment and inventory themselves.

"Amazon profits from outside sellers by taking a percentage commission when their goods are sold," the *Journal* wrote. "Some analysts believe the profit margin is higher on many items sold by outside parties than those sold directly by Amazon." And, of course, it is not tying up any of its own money in making those third-party sales. Because Amazon is such a good example of how to do business today, we will be using it periodically as an example throughout.

But it is not just online companies that generate cash. Many "old economy" companies such as GE, McDonald's, United Technologies, and Berkshire Hathaway are cash generators. GE, for example, has consistently generated cash for twenty-five years. By using automation brilliantly and making its manufacturing ever more efficient, it has reduced its inventory needs and increased its manufacturing capacity.

Invested wisely, cash improves the company's moneymaking ability. Plus there's a psychological component to cash: when a company has its own cash rather than borrowed money, senior managers are more inclined to make bold investments that have greater potential rewards. Amazon's transition from being just an online bookseller to being one of the world's largest retailers is proof of that.

Gross Margin

A key part of cash generation is understanding gross margin. In fact, if you understand gross margin, you are well on your way to understanding the heart of the business. You need to master the anatomy underlying the gross margin of your business.

But before we can talk about gross margin, we need to take a step back to talk about margins in general. Throughout this book, we use the term "margin" to refer to net profit margin. That's the money the company earns after paying its expenses— the costs associated with making and selling the product as well as running the business, making interest payments on any loans, and paying its income taxes.

But "gross margin" occurs a step before that.

Gross margin is calculated by taking the total sales for the company (or a product line) and subtracting the costs directly associated with making or buying it. Those are things such as the cost of the material used to create the products along with the direct labor costs. The "cost of goods sold" (COGS) does not include indirect expenses such as sales and general administration costs or distribution costs.

There is a two-step process to determining your company's gross margin. First, you take your company's total revenues and subtract the cost of goods sold. (You usually don't need to figure it out. It is listed on your company's income statement.) You then divide that figure by revenues to produce a percentage. The formula looks like this:

$$\frac{\text{Revenue} - \text{Cost of Goods Sold}}{\text{Revenue}} = \text{Gross Margin}$$

So if it costs you \$80 in material and labor to produce a product that you sell for \$100, you have a gross margin of 20 percent:

$$\frac{100 - 80}{100} = .20, \text{ or 20 percent}$$

Think back to my family's shoe store. Say our shop sells 1,000 pairs of shoes at \$50 a pair. Our total sales are \$50,000 (\$50 × 1,000). And let's assume the costs directly associated with the shoes are $30,000 ($30 a pair × 1,000 pairs). Our gross margin is $20,000 ($50,000 total sales −$30,000 cost of goods sold = $20,000).

As we saw from the formula, gross margin can also be expressed as a percentage:

$$\frac{\$50,000 \text{ total sales} - \$30,000 \text{ cost of goods sold}}{\$50,000 \text{ total sales}} = .40, \text{ or } 40 \text{ percent}$$

So we could say my family's business has a gross margin of 40 percent.

While the calculation for gross margin is simple, understanding what's behind it is what will make you a great businessperson. What is the product mix, customer mix, pricing mix, mix of distribution channels, and cost structure producing that number? Could any of them be changed to produce a greater gross margin? How about the material and labor costs? Could they be decreased (which would also increase the gross margin)?

Asking questions like this allows you to truly analyze the business. That's why many businesspeople and investors track gross margin—it provides clues about important changes to the business. For example, if your gross margin goes from 52 percent to 48 percent, you have to ask why. Is it costing more to produce your product, or is competition forcing you to lower prices while costs are staying the same? Or is the gross margin declining because the customer mix is changing and you're selling more products that have lower margins and fewer of the high-margin goods? Is the trend going to accelerate?

In the early days of the personal computer, the PC industry

enjoyed gross margins approaching 38 percent. Then came the era of intense competition. The price of a PC fell dramatically, which shaved gross margins dramatically to 12 percent. To survive, PC makers had to change their entire business approach. IBM got out of that business, and Dell went private, which relieved it of the pressure from shareholders to deliver quarterly earnings as it shifted its strategy.

Return on Invested Capital

You might think that making money simply means making a profit. But there's more.

Regardless of size or kind, every business uses its own and/or someone else's money to grow. You borrow from a bank or use your savings. That money represents your capital. The question is, how well do you and your organization employ it?

To discover that, the CEO uses a simple formula in which net income is divided by total capital (your money plus any money you have borrowed):

$$\frac{\text{Net Income}}{\text{Total Invested Capital}} = \text{Return on Invested Capital}$$

The answer gives the number known as return on invested capital (ROIC) or as some people prefer, ROC for return on capital. The greater the number, the better the use of capital.

There is often a perfect correlation between how well a company uses its capital and how its CEO is perceived, as David Trainer—CEO of New Constructs, an independent research firm in Nashville, Tennessee—points out in one of his blogs.

When *Fortune* released its 2016 list of the top fifty businesspeople—which they based on both objective metrics, such as profitability, growth, and shareholder return along with the CEO's leadership and strategic initiatives, Trainer noted a pattern: the top ten CEOs all earned double-digit ROICs.

Executive	Company Name	Ticker	ROIC
Tim Cook	Apple	AAPL	235%
Ajay Banga	MasterCard	MA	118%
Andrew Wilson	Electronic Arts	EA	30%
George Scangos	Biogen	BIIB	30%
Larry Page	Alphabet	GOOGL	26%
Mark Parker	Nike	NKE	25%
Howard Schultz	Starbucks	SBUX	21%
Steve Ells & Montgomery Moran	Chipotle	CMG	17%
Mark Zuckerberg	Facebook	FB	15%
Mary Dillon	Ulta Salon	ULTA	12%

Some people talk about return on equity (ROE), which is a similar calculation but uses only the capital provided by investors who own shares in the company and excludes any debt:

$$\frac{\text{Net Income}}{\text{Shareholders' Equity (assets–liabilities)}} = \text{Return on Equity}$$

Or they use the formula for return on assets:

$$\frac{\text{Net Income}}{\text{Total Assets}} = \text{Return on Assets}$$

> When it comes to gauging the health of the business, a good CEO is not so concerned about precision. She uses return on invested capital (or a similar measure) to get a sense of the business. Is it better than last year and the year before that? Is it better than her competitors' return on invested capital? Is it where it should be? And where is it headed?

Let me prove the point that these simple calculations are easily grasped without formal business education. Many years ago, I took a group of MBA students to an open-air market near Managua, Nicaragua. There merchants (almost all women) sold everything from pineapples to shirts and necklaces.

We approached a woman selling clothing in a small shop, and I asked her how she got the money to pay for her merchandise. She said she borrowed it, paying 2.5 percent interest a month. One fast-thinking student did the math—2.5 percent multiplied by twelve months—and announced that the interest rate was a whopping 30 percent a year. The woman gave me a disapproving look and said in Spanish that the student was wrong. Compounded month to month, the rate was actually 34 percent annually.

How much margin did she make? Just 10 percent. So how could she survive borrowing money from loan sharks charging 34 percent a year? We had to ask.

Annoyed by the stupidity of the question, she made several sweeping circular motions through the air. Her gesture meant rotation—rotation of inventory, or turning the stock over. She knew intuitively that earning a good return had two ingredients—profit margin and velocity. If she sold a blouse for $10, she made just $1 in profit. To pay the interest on the loan and to restock her cart, she had to sell her wares again and again during the day. The more she sold, the more "10 percents" she accumulated.

The word "velocity" describes this idea of speed, turnover, and movement. Think of raw materials moving through a factory and becoming finished products, and think of those finished products moving off the shelves to the customer. That's velocity.

Or picture a grocery store that sells for cash only. Assume that just about all of its capital is invested in the form of inventory. Does the grocer empty her shelves and replace the goods each day, or does it take a week to clear the shelves? The first scenario has higher velocity than the second.

> ## For many companies, inventory velocity is a very revealing number.

Some people use the term "inventory turns" to describe how quickly their inventory moves. It doesn't matter what you call it, because the concept is the same. How many times does the inventory turn over in a year? Walmart has 360 inventory turns in toilet tissue per year. That means the entire inventory of toilet tissue is sold almost every day. Each day, Walmart gets back the money it spent on toilet tissue, plus some profit. That's a terrific use of shelf space and cash.

Figuring out the velocity of any asset requires the same simple arithmetic: your total sales for, say, a year, divided by the value of the asset. If you want to look at inventory velocity, divide total sales by total inventory. But forget memorizing the math. Get the *idea* of velocity. Ask: How long is it from the time an order comes in to the time it is delivered to the customer? How long from the time a company receives raw materials and parts to the time finished product is sold? Things must move through a business to the customer, and the faster the better.

In the United States it takes an average of seventy-two days from the time a new car is ready to be shipped from the plant to the time the consumer drives it off the lot. That whole time, the money used to buy the parts and make the car is tied up. The manufacturer can't get any of it back to use for another purpose until the car reaches the consumer and she pays for it. If the car gets to the consumer sooner, the manufacturer has a lot less money tied up in a product that's sitting on a railroad track or car carrier. That's what I mean by moving faster. That's velocity.

The faster the velocity, the higher the return. In fact, return is nothing more than profit margin multiplied by velocity. This is a universal law of business that can be written simply:

$$\text{Return (R)} = \text{Margin (M)} \times \text{Velocity (V)}$$

Or

$$R = M \times V$$

This simple formula is worth memorizing. You will find $R = M \times V$ to be tremendously useful. The R is stated as a percentage: 8 percent return, 10 percent return, 15 percent return—a single number that can be used for comparison.

Making Velocity Meaningful

Many people focus on profit margin but overlook velocity. Here's what makes successful CEOs different from many other executives: they think about both margin and velocity. This dual focus is the centerpiece of understanding how a business truly works.

> **Focusing on profit margins is good—but insufficient. The best businesspeople, the ones who will be promoted, focus on velocity as well.**

Velocity is important to every company. Consider companies that have a lot of "fixed" assets—factories, machinery, or buildings. Take, for example, AT&T. It has a huge investment in wires, cables, satellites, and microwave towers. With prices for long-distance voice calls falling due to decreased demand (know any college student with a landline in her dorm room?) and margins shrinking in its cellular business (thanks in large part to the intense competition), the only way to improve the return on its invested capital is to focus on velocity.

How? By offering cell service, Internet, and television through its network.

As you hone your business skills, think hard about return on invested capital and its two parts, velocity and profit margin. Look at your own company's return on invested capital and start asking yourself questions. Over the past few years, has the return been improving or declining? How does it compare to your competitors' figures? If it is less, what can you do to improve things? If it is better, ask yourself which companies in any industry have the highest margins, the highest velocity, or the highest return on invested capital. What can you learn from them?

One truth about business is that the return on invested capital has to be greater than the cost of capital itself—that is, the cost of using your own and other people's (banks' and shareholders') money. If the return does not exceed the cost of capital (which is typically 8 percent or more), there will be real discontent among the investors because management is destroying shareholder wealth. Some companies have businesses, divisions, or product lines that do not earn the cost of invested capital. They therefore have to either improve the return or get rid of these lines of business. That's how many CEOs or business unit executives make the decision to sell (divest) a business or discontinue a product line. They are always looking to employ the company's capital as efficiently as possible.

You can help make a difference by suggesting ways to improve the return. If, for example, you work for an automobile company, you'll find the return on small cars is problematic. Auto manufacturers around the world have been earning less than a 2 percent return on them, which is less than the cost of capital. How might that part of the business generate a higher return? Or if you work at a software company, think once again about the formula for return on invested capital:

$$\frac{\text{Net Income}}{\substack{\text{Total Invested Capital (your or your shareholders'} \\ \text{money plus any borrowed money)}}} = \text{Return on Invested Capital}$$

Since the denominator is so small, any way you can figure out to boost net income (earnings) can have a big effect.

Taking a good look into the realities that underlie cash generation, margin, velocity, return on invested capital, and growth provides the clues about where to focus attention and what to change.

Growth

Growth is vital to prosperity. Every person, every company, and every national economy must grow. Are you working for a company that is growing? Is it growing profitably?

If the company is not growing profitably or your business unit lags behind competitors, your personal progress will suffer. You will not have the opportunity to be promoted and move forward. Top managers will begin to cut costs and reduce the number of employees. They'll start reining in R&D and advertising. Good people will leave, and eventually the company will go into a death spiral and employees—including you—will suffer.

| Either you are growing or you are dying.

Today, no growth means lagging behind in a world that grows every day. You can see that in terms of large trends or individual companies. Let's talk about macro trends first.

Been to a record store lately? Drop off any film to be processed? Used a pay phone? Read an afternoon paper (or been able to find a local morning one if you live in a small city, or even a midsize one such as New Orleans)? Bought a printed map? Placed a call from your hotel room through the hotel's phone system? Ordered a set of encyclopedias? Rented a movie from a stand-alone video store like Blockbuster? Used a travel agent to book a routine vacation or business trip? Bought a freestanding GPS unit?

Probably not. And all the companies that used to provide those services are struggling or out of business.

As for individual companies, one might be doing "fine" but be falling behind the competition. It wasn't that long ago that Honeywell and United Technologies were considered equals. Not surprising, since both companies have a large global presence in aerospace and construction. But more recently, Honeywell is doing better—improving margins, integrating acquisitions, and spurring growth.

Doing just "fine" is not enough. United Technologies is falling behind.

Growth has a psychological dimension. Growth energizes a business. A company that is expanding attracts talented people with fresh ideas. It stretches them and creates new opportunities. Employees like to hear customers say they're the best and that more business will be coming their way. They want to be part of a company that is going to be around to shape the future.

Here's proof. In 2015, one in six graduates of Stanford's MBA program started a company once they finished school (and invariably it was one they were working on while they were earning their degree). And if they are not starting companies of their own, an increasing portion of graduates of the top business schools are joining early-stage companies, says John A.

Byrne, founder and editor of PoetsAndQuants, a website that covers the MBA market: "At Harvard Business School, 9% of the graduating class of 2015 went to work for startups that have been in business for three years or less."

What is the attraction? Growth, and all the excitement and opportunities it brings.

Growing the Right Way

Growth for its own sake doesn't do any good. Growth has to be both profitable and sustainable. You want growth to be accompanied by improved margins and velocity, and the cash generation must be able to keep pace. (See the box "What Is Good Growth?") Three stories will underscore the point.

Many entrepreneurs taste success on a small scale and become obsessed with growth, losing sight of the moneymaking basics along the way. Unfortunately, the case of one entrepreneur who served restaurants is typical. He built a profitable business installing beverage equipment at a cost of $2,000 per installation and thereafter collecting $100 a month from the restaurant for the ingredients he supplied.

So far so good. But he borrowed money to make the installations, and the margin on the ingredients was so slim that it did not cover the interest payments. Yet he was obsessed with growth and kept installing his equipment in more and more restaurants. The outflow of cash soon outpaced the flow of money into the business, and the lenders decided that the company needed a new CEO.

Here's story number two. Sometimes senior management

inadvertently encourages unprofitable growth by giving the sales force the wrong incentives. For example, one $16 million injection molding company rewarded its sales reps based on how many dollars' worth of plastic caps they sold; they were not accountable for profits. Everyone was excited when the company landed $4 million of new sales from two major customers, but these large contracts were on slim margins, not enough to generate the cash needed to fund the sales.

Bad growth can take many forms, as this third story shows. To rev up its business in an important unit, a global building company brought in a new division head. He was the heir apparent to the CEO of the parent company and his new assignment was a major test to see if he was ready for the top job.

The new manager believed he could gain significant market share by cutting prices. He was successful—at first. Sales grew over the next three months, and so did the unit's share of the market.

However, the competition responded in kind. Desperate to preserve their market shares to cover their high fixed costs, competitors also cut their prices. The end result? All the price cutting caused revenues, profits, and cash generation to shrink throughout the industry, hurting Global Building along with everyone else.

The parent company had to revise its earnings estimates downward three times in the following twelve months, and it took the *next* division head two years to stabilize the situation.

WHAT IS GOOD GROWTH?

Companies that thrive over the long run grow both the top and bottom lines consistently over time. They do it through good growth.

Good growth is profitable, organic, differentiated, and sustainable. Let's look at all four factors:

- **Profitable.** Good growth has to be not only profitable but capital efficient—that is, it needs to earn an amount greater than the company could receive by putting its money in something ultrasafe like a Treasury bill.
- **Organic.** The best growth naturally flows out of what the company is already doing. Not only is that efficient, but it also builds the organization's creativity muscles.
- **Differentiated.** You never want to provide a product or service that is seen as a commodity. Customers must prefer it. Otherwise, you will never make very much money.
- **Sustainable.** You are not looking for a quick spike in revenues. The goal is to have the growth continue year after year.

Growth Alone Does Not Equal Success

Bankruptcy is often the sad end of misguided expansion plans.

Don't use size as a measure of success. Pushing for more sales isn't necessarily good business. You have to know how and why you're growing. And you have to consider whether you are growing in a way that can continue.

Look at what is happening to your cash. Maybe sales are increasing but the cash situation is getting worse. Step back and figure out what is going wrong. Could it be that your profit margins are shrinking? If so, why?

But if sales are growing and the cash is growing, too, you have some interesting choices. You, or your company, can use the funds to develop a new product, buy another company, or expand. Maybe you could ease prices (without igniting a pricing war) to increase demand profitably, so you'll grow even faster.

Finding opportunities for profitable growth when others can't is a key skill that you need to learn.

Sam Walton is the classic example. The founder of Walmart knew how to grow a business, even when his industry peers thought it was impossible. In 1975, the CEO of Sears Roebuck told my class at Northwestern that retailing in the United States was a mature, no-growth business. That's why he diversified into financial services. Meanwhile, Walton was opening new stores while maintaining a return on capital substantially above the industry average.

The rest, as they say, is history. Walmart recorded nearly half a *trillion* dollars ($485.7 billion) in sales and earned $16.4 billion in 2015, and it is getting better at mastering e-commerce. Sears, which long ago divested its financial services division, struggles to survive, reporting its eleventh straight quarter loss in 2015. Its revenues in 2015 were $25 billion and it lost more than $1 billion.

Opportunities for profitable growth may not be obvious, especially for big, established companies. But with drive, tenacity, and a willingness to take risks, you and your colleagues can discover them.

Where do you look? Think like the CEO and ask, "How do we make money, and can we be profitable giving customers what they want?" From there look at your business from end to end. No matter what you do, it will probably divide into two parts:

1. Everything your company does to produce its product or service
2. Everything it does to sell it

Look at both parts to find the opportunity.

The Growth Box Can Help

One of the best ways to help you spot opportunities is filling in what I call the growth box.

Draw the following:

THE GROWTH BOX

	EXISTING CUSTOMER	NEW CUSTOMER
NEW NEEDS	**B** Existing customers with new needs	**C** New customers with new needs
EXISTING NEEDS	**A** Existing customers with existing needs	**D** New customers with existing needs

Thinking about the four quadrants can trigger ideas for increasing revenues profitably. Let's use some examples to show how.

In Box A (existing customers with existing needs) you are literally trying to expand the pond in which you fish for business by redefining what you do for a living to be more inclusive, while still remaining true to your core. This is what big-box retailers do all the time. General retailers such as Target added groceries in an attempt to get a greater share of their customers' wallet. The home improvement chains, including Home Depot and Lowe's, offer to connect you to contractors who install what you buy. Thinking about Box A can help you a great deal in identifying an adjacent market you can serve with your core competencies.

In Box B (existing customers with new needs), you look for places where neither you nor your competitors are solving a customer problem. Here you are acting like an anthropologist. You are observing the behavior of your customers (and potential customers) to determine what they want. This is what Toyota did in creating Lexus. It observed that its traditional customers were moving upscale, so the automaker created a car that was better than a Cadillac and had more value than a Mercedes (that is, it cost less but was just as good) to satisfy their customers' changing needs.

With Box C (new customers with new needs), you're thinking about going into a new business. This may be the first place you turn when your current strategy is in trouble or if a sudden change in the marketplace has rendered your old strategy obsolete. Nokia once sold more cellphones than anyone. But after being bought by Microsoft in 2014, the company has been focusing on selling high-end networking equipment and software to telecommunications companies.

Avon is a great example of Box D (new customers with existing needs). It identified a new customer segment, teenagers, who had the same concerns about looking their best as its traditional customer base, women in their twenties and older. Having recognized this new customer segment, Avon then set out to serve them through existing capabilities—the traditional "Avon ladies," its catalogs, and its website.

As you see, the growth box is a simple, effective tool to try to spot new opportunities. You only need to ask four questions:

- How can we fill an existing need our current customers have? (Box A)

- What new needs can we satisfy for our customers? (Box B)

- Should we go after new customers who have new needs? (Box C)

- How can we sell what we have to new customers? (Box D)

4

THE TOTAL BUSINESS

*If you and your company are going to succeed,
you need to truly understand the business.*

Having laid out the basics in the last chapter, let's now apply them to your business. (After all, your CEO is most interested in how well you understand the way things work in *your* company.)

The elements of moneymaking we have discussed—customers, cash generation, return on invested capital, and growth—can all be measured. But you don't just want to memorize the ways to do it. What you really want to do is:

A. Understand deeply all four building blocks of a profitable organization

B. Know how to combine them to create a mental picture so you can figure out how well any organization—but especially yours—is doing

> **A true businessperson masters the relationships among customers, cash generation, return on invested capital, and growth to get an intuitive grasp of the total business.**

Someone who truly understands the business knows that if a company continuously improves productivity, then margins increase and cash is generated. When margins and velocity both improve, you have the leeway to make things better for customers, and thus you can get a larger share of the market and your company grows.

This has always been the case, as the Ford Motor Company archives and the book *The Public Image of Henry Ford,* by David L. Lewis, prove. Henry Ford had an intuitive sense of how his total business made money. Knowing what was important to customers, Ford not only made legendary breakthroughs in manufacturing, basically inventing the large-scale industrial assembly line, but reduced the price of his then revolutionary cars every year from 1909 to 1915.

Ford seemed to understand that lower prices and higher wages had a relationship that contributed to moneymaking. In 1914, Ford announced that his company would pay workers a minimum of $5 a day. The wage hike was huge—workers were making $2.34 daily, comparable to wages at other automakers, when he made the announcement, so he was more than doubling their pay.

Higher wages gave more people the wherewithal to buy a car. A French scholar summed it up, writing that the $5-a-day wage "made every worker a potential customer." More customers meant more revenue and profits and therefore more freedom to lower prices. Lower prices made cars affordable for even more people, and so on.

Another story further illustrates Henry Ford's business acumen. In 1916, the Dodge brothers, who owned a stake in Ford, sued because they wanted the company to pay higher dividends. During the court case, their attorney challenged Henry Ford's approach to running the business. The attorney questioned how the owners—that is, the shareholders—could benefit if Ford continued to "employ a great army of men at high wages, reduce the selling price of your car, so that a lot of people can buy it at a cheap price, and offer everybody a car who wants one."

Ford loved the way the attorney described his business. His reply to what was supposed to be an insulting question? "If you give all that, the money will fall into your hands; you can't get out of it."

Henry Ford knew that Ford Motor Company had a winning formula. The elements of moneymaking—customers, cash generation, return on invested capital, and growth—and the relationships between those four elements created a robust business that could continue to make money.

Henry Ford had fun making money. That same sense of fun and excitement can be yours if you start applying the universal laws of business to your company.

Start Here

Begin with the basics of moneymaking. Then try to get a feel for how they work together. Look at your company through the eyes of a street vendor. You probably know a lot about your company—for example, the kinds of products or services it sells, how many manufacturing facilities it has, who your largest customers and vendors are. This tends to be common knowledge at most companies. A street vendor knows similar things—his suppliers, for example, are the people who supply the fruit he sells.

But now the difference between the street vendor and most people in business emerges. See if you can answer the following six questions about your company's sales, margins, velocity, return on invested capital, cash generation, and market share. To make it easier to keep track, here's a table you can fill out. The table may also help you to visualize how your business really works.

Your Company's	Increasing	Decreasing	Flat	Why
Sales				
Gross Margin				
Not Profit Margin				
Velocity				
Return on Invested Capital				
Cash Generation				
Market Share				

Let's go through the questions.

- **What were your company's sales in the last twelve months?** Is your company growing? Are your revenues increasing, flat, or declining? What is the trend? What is going to happen to that growth in the future? As long as it is profitable growth, growth is good. It shows you are serving your customers. But is that growth good enough? You can answer that by looking at how your company's growth rate compares to your competitors' growth rates. Who are the most critical customers? Is that likely to change?

- **What is your company's gross margin?** Is it growing, declining, or flat? How is it going to change in the coming months and years? How does your gross margin compare with competitors'?

- **What is your company's net profit margin?** Is it increasing or decreasing? And what is the relationship between margin and sales growth? Increasing sales along with shrinking margin could be a sign of trouble. Is your customer mix changing? Or your product mix? What is driving the change, up or down?

- **Do you know your company's inventory velocity?** As we talked about in Chapter 3, the faster the better. The faster your products sell, the more quickly you free up cash (while simultaneously reducing the risk that you will be stuck with obsolete products). No matter what that number is, is it growing, flat, or declining? How is it compared to your competitors' numbers? Why? What products/services sell faster than others? Do you know why? What can you do to improve the slower movers? Do you have obsolete inventory? Is the amount of obsolete inventory decreasing? Increasing?

- **What is your company's return on invested capital (ROIC)?** If you know the margin and the velocity, you can figure this out by using the formula $R = M \times V$. Once you know the number, compare it to your company's past performance and that of your competition. Is the ROIC increasing, falling, or staying the same? What can you do to increase your company's performance?

- **Is your company's cash generation increasing or decreasing?** Why is it going one way or the other? What is the trend? And how is your company doing compared to the companies you compete against? What can you do to improve that figure?

- **Is your company gaining or losing share against the competition?** Over the long term, markets tend to get bigger. Your company has to grow just to keep up with that expansion, or your share of the market will shrink. As we have seen, current employees get more excited about working for a growing company. And good people want to join a firm that is dominating and reshaping its industry. Conversely, no one likes to work for an organization that is just treading water or is actually going backward. If the company is going the wrong way, the best people tend to leave first—which just hastens the decline.

How Did You Answer?

If you can answer these questions about your company, you are speaking the universal language of business. You're getting a picture of your company's *total business,* the kind of picture a shopkeeper or a street vendor would have. And, as you just saw, it doesn't take a lot of numbers to get there. You don't need to go deeper than the questions we just asked.

Let's say your company is a net cash generator and its margins are very good compared with your competitors, but low compared with other industries, and your sales growth is not as good as you would like and velocity is low. What would you do? Would you have a better sense of what to focus on? You could look for ways to improve customer satisfaction or increase productivity. You might focus on developing exciting new products and work hard to launch them quickly. And you might make extra efforts to ensure that big investments are made in areas where the business is growing profitably.

Now let's say you work for a firm that has okay margins, its inventory velocity is fantastic, and return on invested capital is great. The company is growing and although market share is increasing, it's still small compared to the share your two biggest competitors have.

Greater market share would be a big help in competing against the two giants. How does this total picture of the business help focus your attention? Would it spur you to look for ways to improve market share through new products and services?

If you work for a public company, ask your investor relations department for the information you need to answer all the questions we asked about sales, margin, velocity, and the like. The numbers are also available now on most companies' websites. For public companies, you can also get this information from the annual report, and online from the U.S. Securities and Exchange Commission (https://www.sec.gov/edgar/searchedgar/webusers.htm). If your company is publicly traded, none of this information is confidential. Your asking for it will demonstrate to management your keen desire to think beyond silos and your willingness to try to help the total business.

If you work for a private company, talk to people in your finance department. In my work with private companies, I have found that management is increasingly willing to share this information. Employees want to know how well the company they work for is doing. And if management wants to hold on to good employees, it must tell them.

Bring your desire to their attention. They are likely to react positively. Maybe this book will encourage them to share that financial information more often. There is less and less reason not to. The company's key customers probably already have this information—companies, especially big companies, want to know that the private firms they deal with are in good financial shape—and competitors probably have a good handle on the numbers as well. Management of a private company probably won't tell you things like how much the CEO is being paid, and other numbers that are closely held. But the fact is, financial information about private companies is not as private as it was fifteen years ago.

And whether you work for a company that is public or private, maybe you can persuade your bosses that the universal language of business does not belong in the executive suite alone. Cash generation, margin, velocity, return on invested capital, growth, and the like should be part of everyone's vocabulary. Remind them that employees can contribute more when they know what really goes on in the business and can apply what they know.

PART II

BUSINESS ACUMEN IN THE REAL WORLD

5

REAL-WORLD COMPLEXITY: SETTING THE PATH AND THE PRIORITIES

Focus. Focus. Focus.

You now know something about the world of the street vendor, the world of CEO, and how those two worlds are similar. Now let's take a closer look at the CEOs. Whether they run small, medium, or large companies, the best ones know how to use the savvy of the street vendor to cut through the complexity of their businesses. They use their business acumen, which is a fancier term for what our fruit vendor would call street smarts, to define a path to take the business forward, and they determine clear, specific priorities, or action items, that will make money and create wealth for their stockholders or owners.

Keep business basics in mind to cut through complexity and set the right path and priorities. Superior CEOs take care to define three priorities that will, in combination, take the business where they want it go, and devote nearly all their time and attention to those priorities. They also use those priorities as a guide for directing resources.

Why so few priorities? In a word, focus. A business priority defines the most important action that needs to be taken at a given point. Many companies have too many priorities and so their focus is split, and the organization ultimately suffers. Not surprisingly, choosing the right priorities is an intense mental exercise, given the degree of complexity.

Every business—whether we are talking about old, traditional companies such as the automaker General Motors or new Internet-based ones such as Lyft, the ride-sharing company—has an enormous amount of it.[1]

General Motors, for example, is one of world's largest companies, with revenues of $152 billion (as of 2015) and 216,000 employees. It produces 10 million vehicles a year (that's about 27,400 each day) in thirty-seven countries under thirteen nameplates, including Chevrolet, Buick, GMC, Cadillac, Holden, Opel, and Vauxhall, selling in nearly every country around the globe (exceptions are North Korea, Cuba, Iran, Sudan, and Syria). It operates 396 facilities on six continents, each of which has its own economic picture, currencies, consumer trends, competitive dynamics, and social concerns. And that complexity is just at the macro level. On top of that, think about how many different ways a car can be configured, from color combinations and the number of doors to trim packages and accessories. GM has dozens of competitors worldwide—not just other car manufacturers but also banks and credit unions, which compete with GM Financial, its automotive financing company.

---

1   It is interesting to underscore here, as we have throughout, how traditional companies are adjusting to the new way of doing business. GM has invested $500 million in Lyft, and as this book goes to press the two companies are in a joint project to test a fleet of self-driving Chevrolet Bolt electric taxis (made by GM) on public roads.

Overlay on this complexity two other considerations that are totally uncontrollable and unpredictable—currency valuations and interest rates—and you have an idea of the things that GM CEO Mary Barra grapples with every day.

Despite the complexity, Barra must be clear about what matters most. GM's priorities might be these:

1. Given that the automotive market is radically changing because of things like ride-sharing, self-driving cars, and the use of algorithms and artificial intelligence, she needs to redesign the company to take advantage of the technologies that can help to design cars faster and serve customers better.
2. She needs to find the right partners going forward. (We'll discuss one such partner, Lyft, next.)
3. And then she needs to combine points 1 and 2 to execute on the redesign of the firm.

Similarly, CEO Logan Green must sort through a similar complexity at San Francisco–based Lyft, the privately held transportation company he runs. The company's mobile-phone application facilitates peer-to-peer ride sharing by connecting passengers who need a ride with drivers who have a car.

Think about what is involved. Not only do you have to design an app that allows people to summon a car from any mobile device anywhere, but you need another one for the drivers, and the two need to sync. In addition, you must create an algorithm that tracks all the drivers available at a given moment in order to determine which driver is closest to the pickup location. Then you have to account for all kinds of options: Does the passenger want a standard car, SUV, or limo? Is she willing to share the ride with someone else? (And if yes, you need to pair passengers who are going in the same general direction.) Is this a corporate account or personal? You get the idea.

In addition, you need a way to find and vet drivers, a simple way for drivers to calculate charges and track what they are owed. On top of all that, management must follow what its main competitor, Uber, is doing, anticipate how regulatory bodies will respond when Lyft wants to enter a market (cab and limousine companies might be major contributors to local politicians and don't want additional competition, and each country has its own rules), and anticipate changing demand (for example, at some point riders will want to summon driverless cars, hence the joint project with GM).

This Is What the Best CEOs Do

Superior CEOs use their business acumen to test the logic of their priorities and the path they are setting the business on. They consider what will happen to the company's moneymaking as a result by revisiting the basics—customers, cash, return on invested capital, and growth—as they shape the future. That focus on the fundamentals helps them discover any flaws and gives them confidence that they are going in the right direction.

It also helps them spot moneymaking opportunities by taking what already exists and combining it in a different way to fill a customer need.

Take, for example, Steve Jobs and the invention of the personal computer. The necessary components—the monitor, disk drives, mouse, keyboard, microprocessors, software, and printer—all existed in the mid-1970s. The seeds had been planted, yet Apple caught the office-automation giants like Wang and Digital Equipment off guard when it introduced its first computer in 1976.

Jobs, working with Steve Wozniak, had the ability to see the moneymaking potential of a machine that promised independence and freedom. No venture capitalists were needed to get Apple off the ground. It made money in its first month and hit a billion dollars in sales within ten years. Today revenues are well over $200 billion and the company's net profit margins average 20 percent.

Think about reducing complexity to simplicity as a brain teaser. There are internal things and external things to consider, and for each of those variables—things like foreign exchange, interest rates, government regulation, and market trends— there's the present status as well as projections about the future. Look at the big picture and see how the variables might come together. Then consider how the moneymaking fundamentals will work with one another, given what you think will happen.

Say you're a marketing manager in charge of four product lines—laundry soaps, dish detergents, toothpaste, and household cleansers. Do you really know which of your product lines makes money? Which one makes the most? Which one makes the least? Do you know which consume cash and which ones generate it? Is one product line more volatile than the others— that is, does demand fluctuate and/or is it subject to intense competition and/or massive discounting?

You should know these things, just as the street vendor knows his apples from his oranges and the margins on each and what is selling the most, so you can always be prepared to respond to changing market conditions. (And, even better, anticipate change.)

Maybe you're an engineer designing a new product. How does it fit into the company's total moneymaking picture? Will the design please customers *and* earn a good margin? Does it have the features many customers want? Do customers prefer it to your competitor's offering? Is it going to require new equipment and thus consume cash?

If your design uses existing equipment, it conserves cash. If you get more sales using the same assets, returns will increase. As an engineer, you can make a contribution by thinking this way—exercising your understanding of how the business really works.

Maybe you're in sales. You generate a lot of business by selling to large customers. But they negotiate hard. They want big discounts and even better payment terms—ninety days instead of the usual forty-five. Try using your business smarts to figure out how to create value for the customer without hurting profitability. If, for example, you are selling to a company like Walmart, maybe you can find a way to increase the velocity of your products on their shelves. The faster the products sell, the faster Walmart recoups its investment. If you can create faster velocity, Walmart benefits without you having to offer additional discounts. These kinds of solutions show that you have street smarts; you are using the business acumen of a street vendor.

> **Everyone in the company should have to take a one-week course that covers the business fundamentals, so they understand how the company makes money.**

Chances are you will face more complexity and volatility as you take on more responsibility. Practice using the tools we have shown you so you will have the courage to face complexity. Many business leaders falter because they become overwhelmed or indecisive. Some do not set clear priorities, or they lose focus. If the CEO fails to set priorities, keeps changing her mind, or communicates poorly what she has decided, the organization loses its energy.

If, on the other hand, she sets business priorities and explains them clearly and often, people will have a better sense of what to do. If she chooses the right set of business priorities, the business will flourish.

In some cases, CEOs succeed for a while because they can engineer mergers and acquisitions and weave persuasive stories for Wall Street securities analysts. These CEOs are known as deal makers. They assemble assets.

More than once I've heard a member of a company's board of directors say, "Sure, he understands Wall Street, but can he really convert these high-price acquisitions into higher growth and high returns?" In many cases, serial asset assemblers were replaced by leaders who focused on business basics and followed the principle of choosing three priorities.

The CEO of a U.S.-based pharmaceutical company is a case in point. Wall Street praised the man highly for engineering the purchase of a European drug company. The two companies had complementary strengths and would become a powerhouse globally. Investors were pleased—but not for long. Soon after the companies were merged, investors began to discover that deal making is one thing, business acumen another. The CEO did not set clear business priorities for the new company, so redundant activities and functions did not get eliminated quickly enough, and the two companies had problems coordinating their marketing efforts. The hoped-for benefits—higher sales, better profitability, and reduced costs—were not materializing. The board asked the CEO to resign in favor of a leader who focused on the priorities that were key to moneymaking.

This scenario has been repeated many times.

6

FROM MAKING MONEY TO CREATING WEALTH

*Your company's price/earnings ratio is the
key for turning money into wealth.*

The CEO of a publicly traded company—I will talk about private companies in a minute—must do more than make money for his organization. Shareholders (and that includes employees who receive stock, or stock options, as part of their compensation) expect a CEO to create *wealth* for them as well.

The best CEOs understand that moneymaking and wealth creation are linked through what is known as the price–earnings multiple. (Also called the P/E multiple or P/E ratio; people usually just refer to it as P/E.)

The "P" is the price of an individual share of stock. The "E" is earnings per share, how much profit the company made per each share of stock.

Written as a ratio, it is:

$$\frac{P \text{ (price of one share)}}{E \text{ (earnings of one share)}} = \text{Price-Earnings Ratio, or P/E}$$

More often it is written as a single number, the result of dividing the P by the E. So if a stock is trading at $30 per share and the company earned $2 per share last year, it has a P/E of 15 (30 divided by 2). Don't worry about the calculation. You can get the exact number for your company from people in your finance department, or from the stock tables in the *Wall Street Journal*, or countless financial websites.

> **A company's P/E ratio has a true multiplier effect. It really can turn money into wealth.**

Here's what's important. The P/E is far from simply a mechanical calculation. A P/E of 15 means that for every dollar of earnings per share, the stock is worth fifteen times that much. Obviously, the higher the P/E multiple, the more wealth is created. And the numbers can get very big, very fast. Take, for example, a company such as Starbucks, which has demonstrated a long history of continuous growth and expanding margins. As I write this, it has a P/E of 36, which means that for every dollar it earns, $36 of wealth is created for its shareholders, many Starbucks employees among them.

The P/E represents expectations about a company's current and future moneymaking ability—the combination of expected cash generation, margin, velocity, return on capital, and profitable revenue growth—vis-à-vis the competition and going forward. In other words, it is a judgment about the company's management. Most often, it is based on a track record and on investors' confidence that management will be able to sustain the moneymaking formula. And it doesn't exist in a vacuum. Investors look at a company's performance and compare it to the market as a whole and to its competitors.

P/E multiples vary from company to company and from industry to industry. (Yahoo is particularly good at displaying that information: https://biz.yahoo.com/p/sum_conameu .html). Plus it can change over time. P/E ratios have been known to plummet when companies miss their moneymaking goals. Any inconsistency calls into question the predictability of cash generation, margin, velocity, return on invested capital, and growth. Investors hate uncertainty. On the other hand, P/E multiples can be enhanced by management delivering on moneymaking commitments consistently and predictably, quarter after quarter. Investors love that and they bid up the P/E accordingly.

This Applies to Private Companies, Too

Even if your company is privately held, the same principles apply. Public scrutiny creates an extra incentive for good discipline, but private companies can create their own discipline. Doing the right things day in and day out builds value. Remember, private companies often get sold or go public: their value is determined by the same principles that underlie the P/E multiple.

That raises this question: where exactly does the P/E come from? For public companies, market forces, based on the assessments of individual investors and securities analysts, deter-

mine a company's P/E. Securities analysts and investors decide
what they think is the appropriate P/E for the companies they
track. They often look at earnings estimates.[2] If their assessment shows the company deserves a higher P/E than the market reflects, their firms tend to buy the stock. The opposite is
also true: they tend to sell if they believe the P/E multiple is
too high.

It's not unusual for two securities analysts to have contra-
dictory recommendations, because their conclusions involve
some degree of judgment. But the key word in that sentence is
"some." Securities analysts do use fixed guidelines and typically
judge the company against other firms in its industry, and they
compare the industry to the total market.

> **A company's stock price and P/E mul-
> tiple evolve as securities analysts and
> investors continually reassess the value
> of the company.**

A common comparison is to look at the individual company
against the Standard & Poor's 500, a collection of five hundred
U.S. companies that are widely held and represent a broad cross
section of the economy. Comparisons like this are telling. Let's
take an example.

While the P/E multiple of the S&P 500 during the summer of 2016 was twenty-four, the P/E of most of the major oil
companies was less than half that for two major reasons. First,

---

2   Try to understand the anatomy of any earnings estimate; your accounting department should be able to help.

worldwide production was increasing while demand was flat, creating an oil glut that was driving down the price of oil. Second, in past periods of slow economic growth, the industry had performed poorly, and fast economic growth was nowhere in sight in the summer of 2016.

P/Es do vary widely within an industry, and that difference can go a long way toward attracting talented employees. People want to be part of fast-growing, exciting companies.

Let me tell you about a millennial I know. Right out of college, Bryan joined one of the world's largest retailers, a Fortune 200 U.S.-based company. (He had worked in one of their stores during college, which helped him get hired.) Even though he was a psychology major from a state school, the company realized during its interviewing process that Bryan had an intuitive understanding of numbers, and that he was both bright and extroverted. They concluded that he should be marked as "high potential" and put through the company's rigorous eighteen-month training program, which exposes future leaders to every part of operations.

Bryan thrived in the program and discovered he loved learning how the company made money. He asked to work on the finance side of the business once he finished the training program.

For the next eleven years he excelled at the retailer, working his way up in the finance department before accepting a lateral transfer to the retail side so he could learn about merchandising. At the age of thirty-four, he found himself in charge of deciding where one of the company's largest divisions should source its clothes and at what price.

But although his career was proceeding smoothly, Bryan

found himself increasingly frustrated. Because he was still considered a high-potential executive, he was invited to sit in (at the back of the room) on meetings at the most senior levels of the company. He could not believe how long it took his boss's bosses to make decisions, and he was frustrated that they would rarely ask people like him, who had direct interaction with suppliers every day, for information on trends and on what was going on in the marketplace.

Bryan knew he wasn't alone in feeling this way. There was a distinct lack of energy in the halls. In talking to his peers, he found out that they, too, didn't think they were able to contribute all they could.

The occasional headhunter had called over the years, and while he had always said he was not interested, Bryan kept their phone numbers. One day he called one he liked and said, "I am not necessarily looking to make a move, but if you hear of a rapidly growing company who could use someone with my skills, I'd be happy to talk."

Four months later, he had joined a physical fitness retailer that was increasing sales profitability 30 percent a year, as the head of global sourcing for its products. It wasn't the raise that got him to move. It was the chance to be part of something that was growing, exciting, and filled with people who couldn't wait to get to work. He took a cut in pay but his compensation was tied to creating value for shareholders. He would have the chance to buy company stock at a 15 percent discount and would get stock options on his first anniversary of joining the firm. Wall Street, too, was excited by the company, which had a P/E in the high 30s, 50 percent higher than the stock market as a whole.

"I am working flat out now," Bryan says. "There are some loooooooooong days. But I can't tell you how satisfying it is to see a direct link between the decisions I make and where the company is going."

Managing the P/E

A higher P/E ratio creates more shareholder wealth. A CEO who truly understands the business fundamentals we have talked about knows that. In fact, he knows it puts even more importance on the moneymaking formula. If the formula is right, the company will make money. And if the company executes that formula consistently over time, the company's profits and P/E multiple will rise.

A publicly held company that grows the top line (sales, or revenues) and the bottom line (profit, or earnings) consistently over time without lowering velocity will increase its P/E multiple. If you increase velocity, that's even better because, as we have seen, a higher velocity gives you a better return on invested capital, one of the things both analysts and investors look at. High velocity also reduces the risk that you will be stuck with inventory that doesn't sell. That lifts the P/E even more, and shareholders become wealthier.

But what happens if the company misses the earnings-per-share expectations, even by a penny or two? The punishment on "the street," shorthand for investment professionals, can be severe.

Consider what happened one day in the spring of 2016. After the stock market had closed for the day, Alphabet, the parent company of Google, reported revenues of $20.3 billion for the quarter that had just ended, matching stock analysts' expectations. But income of $7.50 per share was about 6 percent less than the $7.96 the analysts had predicted. Alphabet's stock fell 5.3 percent the next day, or about $27.4 billion in value.[3]

The situation involving Microsoft that same day was more extreme. It, too, reported quarterly sales (of $22 billion in its case) that analysts were expecting, but it missed the earnings estimate by a mere 2 cents a share (analysts were predicting earnings of 64 cents, and the actual earnings were 62 cents). The stock fell 7 percent as a result, or $31.4 billion.[4]

Why does this kind of stock market reaction happen?

When a company misses expectations or says that earnings are not going to grow as fast as management had forecast, investors begin to question whether the company can deliver on its commitments going forward. And it's not just the stock price that falls. The P/E declines, too.

If the miss in earnings is a temporary thing, the stock will come back. But if the miss is the first in a series of disappointments, things can get worse. And this is not a problem for the CEO alone. If the P/E multiple is depressed, the entire company can be vulnerable. Its ability to buy other companies is signifi-

---

3   Here's where that number comes from. When Wall Street professionals determine the value of a public company, they multiply the company's share price by the number of shares it has outstanding. That number is what is known as the company's market capitalization, or market value. On April 22, 2016, the closing share price of Alphabet, the parent company of Google, closed at $718.77. The previous day it had closed at $759.14, a decline of $40.37, or 5.3 percent. The company had 686.5 million shares outstanding. When you multiply the shares outstanding by the decline of 40.37 per share, you get a drop in market value of 27.4 billion dollars.
4   You calculate the Microsoft loss just as you did Alphabet's. Microsoft closed at $51.78 on April 22, exactly $4 less than it had the day before. The company had 7.8 billion shares outstanding, so the loss was $31.4 billion dollars.

cantly hampered, and instead of being the company that grows, it could become an acquisition target for other companies.

Like any industry, investment bankers have a product line. Theirs is known as mergers and acquisitions. A troubled company might start showing up on an investment banker's radar screen as an underperformer. The banker might then convince another firm that the underperformer would be a bargain to buy if the one company were willing to take on the risk to improve the other's performance. The laggard thus becomes a takeover target.

Indeed, takeovers can take place multiple times for the same company. Here's an example. In the mid-1990s, AMP, the world's largest and most respected manufacturer of electronic components, seemed poised for continued success. The company dominated its sector and sold products used in several industries that were experiencing tremendous growth at the time, including telecommunications and computers. But AMP lost sight of its moneymaking fundamentals and allowed margins, growth, and velocity to decline. As a result, both its stock price and P/E multiple fell. It was acquired by Tyco in 1998.

Tyco set out to fix the underlying problems. It took only a year to make $1 billion in cost reductions, improve the margins and velocity, and get AMP back on a growth trajectory. Tyco's P/E and stock price both went up as a result of that acquisition.

But then Tyco struggled. In 2002, revenues hit nearly $25 billion but the firm lost more than $9 billion. The situation was made worse by a massive scandal involving excesses by its chairman and CEO, L. Dennis Kozlowski, and his senior management team.

Edward D. Breen, the former president and COO of

Motorola, was named Tyco's new president and CEO. Breen gutted the existing board of directors and Kozlowski's leadership team. One month after Breen's appointment, Tyco announced the appointment of John A. "Jack" Krol, the former CEO of DuPont, as chairman of the board. The new board and CEO stabilized the company and brought in Tom Lynch to run AMP, which had been renamed Tyco Electronics. Lynch's major task was getting the Tyco Electronics division ready to be spun off as a freestanding public company.

The first step was to define what the company was to be: a firm that designs and manufactures connectivity and sensor solutions for a variety of industries including automobiles, data communication systems, aerospace, defense, and consumer electronics. He sold off some $2 billion worth of business that did not fit with that definition.

In June 2007, Tyco Electronics became a public company and Lynch worked to make it purely a technology firm. He also got rid of government contracts, increased productivity, and opened manufacturing plants in China.

The company changed its name to TE Connectivity in 2011 to reflect its corporate focus, and its success kept would-be acquirers at bay. In 2015, TE Connectivity had sales of more than $12 billion a year and earnings of $2.4 billion. Its stock price has roughly doubled since 2007.

How to Stay Independent

When mergers and acquisitions take place involving companies such as the old AMP, the financial logic, often based on "synergies," is quite compelling. The merged company can combine or eliminate duplicate distribution facilities, sales forces, and accounting departments. Such synergies usually boil down to cost reductions, at least for a while. The human cost can be very high. It's fun to be a consolidator; it's misery to be a "consolidatee."

Find out what your company's P/E multiple is. How does it compare to those of its peers and the S&P 500? Has your company been focused on consistent, predictable, profitable growth; sustainable sources of cash generation; improved margins and velocity; and thus a solid return on invested capital quarter by quarter? Is your company better than your competitors at those things, and is it improving? If so, your company is in good shape. You may be on the offensive, looking for acquisitions. Chances are you're retaining your star performers and attracting new talent. It feels good to be part of such a thriving business.

Or is your company chronically underperforming and inconsistent in terms of moneymaking basics? Is your company's P/E multiple therefore beginning to decline relative to those of competitors and the S&P 500? Are your bosses and coworkers deeply concerned? Are they facing reality or avoiding it?

Perhaps your company has a high P/E multiple compared with your competitors but a low one compared with companies outside your industry. It may be a sign that investors think your industry has little room for growth. Can your company challenge that no-growth assumption?

Netflix is doing just that, and it's upending television viewing in the process.

Until recently, the only way to get a television program on

the air was to pitch network executives and, if they were intrigued, film a "pilot." If that sample episode tested well, the network would commit to a limited number of shows and say in essence, "Let's see how well they do and then we will think about a second season." Not surprisingly, the people pitching those shows hate the arrangement.

Netflix does things differently. It commits to buying a series based on the pitch—and often gives the creator a two-year deal.

Netflix is doing a second thing differently as well. Having paid huge salaries to stars of movies that didn't do well at the box office (think Tom Cruise in *Eyes Wide Shut* or *Valkyrie*), Hollywood now pays actors less up front and offers part of the profits. While that made it possible for Daniel Craig to make something like $40 million for his work in the hit James Bond movie *Spectre,* many actors lose out. If the film doesn't do well, they make less than they did in the past. In contrast, Netflix gives its stars a huge paycheck up front. It can afford to do that because the company's analytics are remarkably good at predicting which projects their subscribers will like—and, equally important, which ones serve as an inducement to get more new customers to sign up for Netflix's services.

A third thing also bolsters Netflix's growth: because it offers its content through streaming, it can expand very quickly. Ten years after it started, its service was available everywhere in the world except China.

The result? Netflix, which started in 1997, is now 379th on the Fortune 500, with $6.8 billion in revenue and $123 million in profits. It accounts for 6 percent of all television viewing in the United States today, and that number is expected to more than double within five years. Netflix announced it had 89 million paid subscribers worldwide at the end of 2016, up 19 million from the year before.

The point is, you want to think differently. Broaden your definition of consumer needs and seek a better way of fulfilling existing ones. One way to do that is to reframe the way you see the world. Stop looking in the rearview mirror and imagine what will happen in the future.

The Starbucks Example

Let's restate the link between making money and creating wealth. The best CEOs continually improve the fundamentals of moneymaking. The investment community tends to reward such CEOs and companies with a higher P/E multiple, which creates tremendous wealth for shareholders. It creates job security and growth opportunities for employees, and wealth for those who receive stock options.

Take a look at Starbucks, which gives employees stock as part of their compensation. It has a terrific record of creating wealth for its shareholders. It has done so because it understands exactly what it is and what it needs to do.

It was a lesson learned the hard way. After Howard Schultz, the guiding force behind the company—and the man who served as CEO from 1987 to 2000—left, Starbucks lost its way. In a memo to his successor in 2007, Schultz summarized what went wrong. Perhaps the subject line says it best: "The Commoditization of the Starbucks Experience."

Let me share some excerpts. You'll notice the focus is

almost entirely on one of the building blocks of business: taking care of customers and giving them the best experience possible. Indeed, as you will see, he uses the word "experience" throughout. And as you will see, he understands just how difficult it is to implement the building blocks of business successfully.

> Over the past ten years, in order to achieve the growth, development, and scale necessary to go from less than 1,000 stores to 13,000 stores and beyond, we have had to make a series of decisions that, in retrospect, have led to the watering down of the Starbucks experience, and what some might call the commoditization of our brand.
>
> Many of these decisions were probably right at the time, and on their own merit would not have created the dilution of the experience; but in this case, the sum is much greater and, unfortunately, much more damaging than the individual pieces. For example, when we went to automatic espresso machines, we solved a major problem in terms of speed of service and efficiency. At the same time, we overlooked the fact that we would remove much of the romance and theatre that was in play with the use of the La Marzocco machines. This specific decision became even more damaging when the height of the machines, which are now in thousands of stores, blocked the sight line the customer previously had to watch the drink being made, and for the intimate experience with the barista.
>
> This, coupled with the need for fresh roasted coffee in every North American city and every international market, moved us toward the decision and the need for flavor locked

packaging. We achieved fresh roasted bagged coffee, but at what cost? The loss of aroma—perhaps the most powerful non-verbal signal we had in our stores; the loss of our people scooping fresh coffee from the bins and grinding it fresh in front of the customer, and once again stripping the store of tradition and our heritage.

> ## "Every time we raise value for a shareholder, we raise value for our people."
> —HOWARD SCHULTZ, CEO, Starbucks

Then we moved to store design. Clearly we have had to streamline store design to gain efficiencies of scale and to make sure we had the ROI on sales to investment ratios that would satisfy the financial side of our business. However, one of the results has been stores that no longer have the soul of the past. Some people even call our stores sterile, cookie cutter, no longer reflecting the passion our partners feel about our coffee. In fact, I am not sure people today even know we are roasting coffee. You certainly can't get the message from being in our stores.

We desperately need to look into the mirror and realize it's time to get back to the core and make the changes necessary to evoke the heritage, the tradition, and the passion that we all have for the true Starbucks experience.

While the current state of affairs for the most part is self-induced, it has led to competitors of all kinds—small and large coffee companies, fast-food operators, and mom and pops—to position themselves in a way that creates awareness, trial and loyalty of people who previously have been Starbucks customers.

He was understating that last point. In 2007, Starbucks stock fell 50 percent, in large part because of the inroads made by McDonald's, which after decades of offering truly terrible coffee finally put an emphasis on serving good coffee, and by the ever-expanding Dunkin' Donuts chain, known for its superior coffee.

Schultz became CEO again in 2008 and righted the company. And shareholders benefited. During the ten-year period from June 30, 2006, to June 30, 2016, Starbucks's share price basically tripled: it went from $18.99 a share to $57.12, an annual gain of 11.6 percent, and its P/E ratio was 40 percent higher than it had been a decade earlier.

Starbucks consistently delivers results and has realistic programs in place to continue to do so in the future. When investors see that consistency over many years, they begin to think it will continue. As of June 30, 2016, Starbucks had a P/E ratio of 36, compared to 23 for the S&P 500.

In December 2016, Schultz announced he was stepping down again as CEO to concentrate on developing and growing the company's "ultra-premium retail formats." He is being replaced by the company's chief operating officer, Kevin Johnson. A month later, three new directors—from Sam's Club, Microsoft, and LEGO—were nominated to the board. It will be interesting to see what happens to the stock going forward.

What Can You Do?

In this digital age, where millennials already make up one-third of the workforce, every person can think of ideas that can improve profitable growth and generate cash by focusing on the customer and the customer experience. For example, how about figuring out a way to get your product to customers faster? Think about the implications for moneymaking and the P/E multiple if you could do that.

Rethinking how business has traditionally been done can also lead to new avenues of growth.

Opportunities exist for every employee to use her business acumen. Remember, shareholders aren't the only ones who benefit from such wealth creation. Employees, too, stand to benefit from opportunities to earn more, grow more, and avoid the uncertainty of changes imposed from outside because the company has underperformed.

7

PUTTING EVERYTHING TOGETHER: HOW AMAZON MAKES MONEY

By now you understand the handful of things that will determine if your organization—whether you work for a business, a nonprofit, or a government agency—will succeed, and you know the fundamentals don't differ whether you are running a fruit stand or a Fortune 500 company. Every organization must manage its cash effectively, use its assets wisely, constantly improve and grow, and serve its customers. Yes, the complexity is different. But that is not surprising given how much smaller a fruit stand is compared to a Fortune 500 company. (The 500th—that is, the smallest—company on the 2016 list, Burlington Stores, had revenues of more than $5 billion.) However, the basics are the same.

Even though we've covered a lot of ground in talking about how both the street vendor and the CEO run their businesses, by design, we spent a lot of time on a few items. The point is to concentrate on the things that make your company thrive:

1. Taking care of customers
2. Generating cash
3. Earning a good return on invested capital and
4. Growing profitably

All of those have metrics. But numbers, especially when it comes to the way corporations report how well they are doing, can be intimidating, and people tell me they have trouble finding the right ones.

That isn't surprising. To comply with Generally Accepted Accounting Principles (GAAP)—the common standards and procedures companies use to build their financial statements—and various federal reporting regulations, companies generate a slew of numbers. For example, the financial reporting of a relatively simple-to-understand company like McDonald's runs to twenty-eight pages in its most recent annual report. (The summary takes an additional three.)

Fortunately, you don't need to master each line, number, and footnote. In fact, to get an idea of how well a company is being run, you usually only have to look at three sets of fairly straightforward numbers:

- The company's *profit-and-loss (P+L) statement* (sometimes called the income statement), which summarizes revenues and costs.

- The *balance sheet,* which is a summary of the company's assets, liabilities, and shareholders' equity. It is called a balance sheet because assets must always equal liabilities plus shareholder equity—that is, they must balance. And it is not surprising that they do balance, since shareholder equity is nothing more than assets minus liabilities.

- The *cash flow statement,* which tracks the amount of cash entering and leaving the company. People usually refer to this as cash flow. As I said earlier, I prefer to think of it as cash generation, but it is the same concept: the money that flows into the business and the money that flows out.

While those statements can get detailed, there are only in total a dozen or so lines that you need to pay attention to. We will go through them in a minute. Before we do, I want to underscore that the following discussion is especially important for two groups. The first group is millennials, and the reason is obvious: they will be business leaders soon (and for decades ahead), if they understand what we are going to discuss.

The second group is members of the sales force, especially those who sell to other businesses. The nature of business-to-business selling is changing. If you are a B2B salesperson today, you are not selling products. You are selling what will create value for your customers. What do they value? The business-building fundamentals. They want to take care of *their* customers. They want to sell them more. And they want to increase their profit margins and use their capital wisely (by reducing the amount of inventory that they carry, for example). Salespeople have to prove that their product or service can do all those things.

> **If you can show your customers that your product will create more value for them, you will make more sales. And if you show your own company that you understand what will provide more value for it, you will be promoted.**

Okay, on to those dozen or so factors I mentioned. I will use Amazon as our example because most people are aware of the company and what it does.

I am going to be looking at Amazon's numbers for five years—the last three chronologically, as this book went to press, and estimates for the next two. Where do those estimates come from? In this case, from the securities analysts Ali Dibadj and Carlos Kirjner of Sanford C. Bernstein, the investment research and management firm. (Obviously, the better the research—and the research these two did is very good—the better the projections are likely to be.)

With that by way of background, let's take a look at Amazon's financial statements. We will start with a simplified income (P+L) statement.[5] And we will begin our discussion with revenues, which you can see have been growing dramatically and are expected to continue to do so.

---

5   I have stripped out various lines in all three statements you are about to see, just to make the discussion easier to follow. You can find the full P+L, balance sheet, and cash flow statements in Amazon's annual report, http://phx.corporate-ir.net/phoenix .zhtml?c=97664&p=irol-reportsannual. I am only going to include the numbers you need to concentrate on. All the numbers you are about to see have been rounded off.

AMAZON'S INCOME STATEMENT

	2013	2014	2015	2016	2017
REVENUES[6]	74.3	88.9	107.0	136.7	165.8
Cost of Sales	54.1	62.7	71.6	86.9	103.3
Gross Profit	20.2	26.2	35.3	49.7	65.5
Gross Profit Margin	27.2%	29.5%	33%	36.4%	39.1%
OPERATING EXPENSES					
Technology and Content	6.5	9.2	12.5	17.1	22.6
Marketing	3.1	4.3	5.2	7.3	9.6
General and Administrative Expenses	1.1	1.6	1.7	2.2	2.8
NET INCOME	.273	(.241)	.6	2.8	5.6

6   All numbers are in $ billions unless otherwise indicated.

Why are these numbers in the P+L statement so important? Think back to our discussion in Chapters 2 and 3 when we were talking about what the CEO wants you to focus on. Remember what the first one was? Customers. Why? Because if you don't have a customer, you don't have a business.

The dramatically growing revenue line shows that Amazon CEO Jeff Bezos is relentlessly focused on the customer. He is always pushing employees to make Amazon faster, less expensive, and more convenient for its customers, and those efforts continue to pay off. Consumers are responding to one-click ordering and same-day delivery (available in some markets), and they love Amazon Prime, which provides exclusive access to movie and television shows, ad-free music, unlimited storage of photos, and free two-day shipping. The selection, price, and convenience are what is driving the revenue line higher.

Staying with the P+L statement, take a look at gross margins. You'll recall the two-step process in figuring it out. In step one, you take your company's total revenues and subtract the cost of goods sold. (In the table, the Bernstein analysts refer to this as "cost of sales.") You then divide that figure by revenues.

Here's the formula we first saw in Chapter 3:

$$\frac{\text{Revenue} - \text{Cost of Goods Sold}}{\text{Revenue}} = \text{Gross Margin}$$

A quick glance tells you that Amazon's gross margin is steadily increasing. Now let's try to understand what is behind that number.

Amazon is progressively moving to sell groceries, a notoriously competitive business. That would certainly further cement its relationship with customers, but it would shrink the margins. What is going to offset that and produce the dramatically higher gross margins the analysts are projecting? My guess is selling even more Amazon Prime memberships. Bernstein estimates that there were between 58 and 69 million Prime subscribers worldwide—who paid $86 on average in 2015 to be members of Amazon Prime. That works out to between $5 billion and $6 billion in revenue gained. Bernstein added, "We conclude a Prime user addition will ultimately generate incremental operating profit of $115 per user per year." Selling private-label goods, or goods that carry the Amazon name, could boost margins as well.

There is one huge takeaway from Amazon's gross margin: the more it grows, the more cash the company generates.

Place Your Bets

Next, a big number to look at in Amazon's case is its investment in technology. Clearly, this is where the retailing battle is going to be fought going forward, as every company tries to predict customer needs and figure out the fastest and least expensive ways to deliver goods. In 2016, only about 8 percent of total U.S. retail sales were e-commerce transactions, according to S&P Capital IQ. But that number is growing at 10 percent a year, far faster than retail as a whole, and Amazon had a majority of the growth in U.S. e-commerce sales in 2016.[7] So if you are a retailer, you need to make technology spending a priority, as Amazon is doing today and is expected to continue to do going forward.

> **Amazon is a technology company—from the platform on which you order what you want to the automation of its warehouses. It is now the Google of retailing. Its spending on technology reflects that.**

Every business has one or two drivers that will determine its success in the future. You want to see that the company is

---

7   "Amazon Accounts for 43% of US Online Retail Sales," *Business Insider*, February 3, 2017; http://www.businessinsider.com/amazon-accounts-for-43-of-us-online-retail-sales-2017-2.

investing in what will keep it competitive—and, you hope, more than competitive—and create value for the customer and the corporation. (As you will see when we discuss Amazon's earnings, the company is not overly interested in making large profits; it is spending most of what it earns to grow.)

Competitors have taken notice. Walmart, for example, spent $3.3 billion to buy Jet.com, an online retailer, in 2016; that followed its announcement in late 2015 that it would spend $2 billion to upgrade its technology over the next twenty-four months.

When Less Is More

While you want to see the same or more spending every year in the areas that are pivotal to the company's growth, conversely you also want to see that a company is keeping a tight rein on general and administrative expenses. This is corporate overhead, which includes the costs of running the head office and its warehouses, paying for the company's accountants and lawyers, and making sure the organization is in compliance with all government regulations. This figure can be as high as 20 percent of revenues at some companies. As the income statement shows, it is a fraction of that at Amazon, at 1.6 percent. That's further confirmation that the company is focusing on the things that really matter—in this case keeping overhead low so there is more money to invest in satisfying customers.

On a related note, you also want to take a look at sales and marketing expenses. If you are a consumer products company, as Amazon is, you need to reach consumers, and that means spending money on marketing.

As you examine how much a company spends to reach its

audience, you want to make sure it is sufficient (the easiest way to do that is to compare the company you are examining to its peers), and you also want to make sure it is consistent over time. If marketing is important to the company's success today, it should be important next year as well. Amazon's income statement clearly shows a steady increase in marketing spending as the company grows.

That brings us to profits. As you can see, accounting-driven profit is not something Jeff Bezos really cares about. He cares about cash per share of stock. Why is profit so low? Because he is hiring top-notch software engineers, computer scientists, and the like. While those experts will build the company's future and we might think of their high salaries as an investment, for accounting purposes, their salaries must be listed as an expense, and therefore profits are lower. You can see that same sort of thing when you turn to the balance sheet and look at accounts receivable and accounts payable.

AMAZON'S BALANCE SHEET

	2013	2014	2015	2016	2017
ASSETS					
Cash, Cash Equivalents, and Marketable Securities	12.4	17.4	19.6	25.1	34.9
Accounts Receivable	4.1	4.7	6.5	7.1	8.7
Total Assets	40.1	54.5	65.4	81.2	103
LIABILITIES					
Accounts Payable	15.1	16.4	20.4	24.5	30.3
Long-term Debt	7.4	15.6	16.1	21	24.3
Total Liabilities	30.4	43.7	52	61.6	73.6
SHAREHOLDERS' EQUITY	9.7	10.7	13.3	19.5	29.3

Accounts receivable is the money owed the company. Accounts payable is what the company owes. The table shows that accounts payable is consistently greater than accounts receivable. The company has a relatively small figure for accounts receivable, because people pay for what they order immediately. But Amazon has negotiated great terms with its suppliers, who give the company lots of time to pay its bills—let's say seventy-two days. That means you, as an Amazon customer, pay for your item(s) on the day you order it, day one. But Amazon has the use of that cash for seventy-one days, until it has to pay its supplier for the item. The cash flow statement captures the virtue of this business model: the more Amazon grows, the more cash it generates.

AMAZON'S CASH FLOW STATEMENT

	2013	2014	2015	2016	2017
NET CHANGE IN CASH	8.6	14.5	15.9	21.7	31.6

When we look at cash and shareholders' equity on the balance sheet, we see that Amazon is in solid shape. Assets are greater than liabilities, and shareholders equity (assets minus liabilities) is rising, which is good. After all, shareholders' equity is a shorthand phrase for the net book value of the company.

And that brings us to the one thing that the street vendor concentrates on the most: cash on hand. In a company like Amazon it is not just a pocketful of $20 bills. It includes "cash equivalents," which are things like U.S. Treasury bills, bank certificates of deposit, money market funds, and marketable securities (bonds and common stock)—just a more complex version of the same basic measure.

What Have We Learned?

These relatively few numbers are really all you need to look at to get a good understanding of the financial shape of Amazon, or any other company.

> **In the same way a doctor uses certain measurements like your pulse, blood pressure, and weight to help diagnose your health, an organization's financials can help you diagnose the health of your company—or any company.**

You can see Amazon is taking care of the business fundamentals—the numbers show it is serving its customers, growing profitably, and using its money wisely. Indeed, it is a cash machine. If its success continues, it will generate even more cash, which it can use to experiment, take risks, and come up with new products, services, and approaches to satisfy its customers even more.

Now that you know what to look for in Amazon (and all other companies, including your own), you need to keep an eye on trends. If things change, you need to ask why. If the company stops growing, again you need to ask why. If it begins gobbling cash, what's the reason?

These are the sorts of things the CEO wants you to know.

PART III

AN EDGE IN EXECUTION

8

EXPANDING CAPACITY THROUGH FLAWLESS EXECUTION

Execution: the art and discipline of getting things done.

Each of us can practice what CEOs with superb business understanding do instinctively: use the universal laws of business, as they set the path and select the right priorities, so the organization can grow profitably.

But understanding how to make money is one thing. Making it happen, getting it done, executing it—that's something else.

As every CEO knows, in business there are milestones that occur annually, quarterly, weekly, and even daily, but there are no finish lines. Leaders have to deliver results day in, day out, relentlessly and consistently. Delivering results is what gives an organization energy, builds confidence, and generates resources to go forward.

Assume you've determined three business priorities that together create a powerful moneymaking machine. How will you actually get the work done? Unless you're a one-person shop, like a street vendor, you cannot personally execute them all. You need the help of other people.

Whether you're a CEO, the head of a department, or someone just starting out in your career and hoping to advance, you must be a leader of the business and a leader of people. *A leader of the business knows what to do. A leader of people knows how to get it done.* A leader of people knows how to harness the efforts of others, expand their personal capacity, and synchronize their efforts. If you do all that, you get results. You'll have an edge in execution.

That's what this chapter is about:

1. Making sure you have the right people to get the work done well.
2. Coaching them so they can expand their personal capacity, in order that they—and the business—can accomplish more.
3. Coaching them on their behavior, so they can become leaders themselves.
4. Understanding what to do when there is a mismatch between the person and the job he or she has been hired to do.

Before we go further, let's stop to make an important point. Being a leader of people is not the same as being a "people person." Think of someone who is good with people. How would you describe that individual? When I ask this question in the classes I teach, people say "outgoing," "well liked," "lots of personality," "enthusiastic," "gets other people excited," "charismatic."

But personality alone is not what makes a company deliver. That takes insight into how the organization really works and the ability to link people's actions and decisions to the right things. In fact, it is this ability that sets the superstar CEOs apart. Without it, many otherwise talented CEOs, not to mention entrepreneurs who have superb business understanding, ultimately fail. The ability to execute and get results through harnessing the abilities of others is how many CEOs have climbed the rungs of the corporate ladder. It is key to your own personal growth and development. It is what gets you promoted.

Gaining an edge in execution takes relentless practice, not just understanding management or leadership in theory. To achieve tangible, measurable results consistently over time, you must be able to select and develop the right people, and then you have to synchronize their efforts and link them to the business's priorities.

The Right People in the Right Jobs

Every business needs the right people in the right jobs. The modern corporation is built on the idea of "professionals" who use their particular talents to help the business succeed. No matter what the job, if the person making decisions is not suited to it, the quality of the decisions could be poor, and the whole company suffers as a result. If the person is well matched to what she is doing, she will get better and better at it, and enjoy her work. More important, her capacity will increase, she will improve even more, and she will be recognized sooner and promoted. If this is repeated throughout the company, the entire business makes huge progress.

> Leaders who deliver results consistently over a long period of time are the ones who recognize what an individual can do best. They link the business need and the person's natural talent. They take the time and effort to place individuals where their strengths can have the most impact.

Matching the person to the job begins with understanding what kinds of skills, attitudes, and aptitudes are required to accomplish the business priorities. You'd be surprised at how often leaders, even the leaders in your company, ignore this.

If you were Sam Walton and you were trying to build your business, how would you select people to run your stores? You would look for employees who truly want to understand the customer and who are fixated on selling reliable goods at a price lower than the competition's. Making money in the retail business means managing margin and inventory velocity and growing volume. If you can't find people who understand that, you will never achieve your dream of becoming a retailing giant.

Sam Walton carefully selected people who met those criteria, and he developed and trained them. Employees were taught to watch revenues, price, inventories, and customers like the proverbial hawk. And they had considerable autonomy to make decisions and take action.

Let's take another example. I talked about Starbucks in Chapter 6. Have you been to a Starbucks? Did you notice the people who make the coffee? Theirs could be perceived as a boring job, but they seem to enjoy it. CEO Howard Schultz's success is, in large part, a result of his ability to recruit, nurture, and develop employees who understand the significance of their work and the company's goal of creating a comfortable "third place" between the office and home. If Starbucks can't get those people—or, as we saw earlier from Schultz's memo, it forgets what's important—the company will begin to deviate from what made it successful, and its fast growth could stall.

Okay, but Walmart and Starbucks are consumer-facing companies, you point out. What kind of people would you need at a company like GE, where CEO Jeff Immelt is transforming the company using an open operating system called Predix as a digital platform for applications that "connect to industrial assets, collect and analyze data, and deliver real-time insights for optimizing industrial infrastructure and operations"? Descriptions of GE's new direction can sound vague, so Immelt simplifies the company's strategy by pointing to a picture of a train.

"We used to call that a locomotive," he said during a speech explaining the new GE. "Now it is a rolling data center. It is filled with sensors and applications. We can monitor fuel performance and increase it. We can learn instantly when a wheel is broken and run the train more safely while increasing utilization."

Predix is part of creating what Immelt calls "the Industrial Internet." How important is it to GE? Sales by GE's Digital Division, which were $5 billion in 2015, are expected to triple by 2020. Why? Because, as the train example shows, the analytics built into the system increase uptime, enhance output and performance, identify trends and anomalies, and allow for remote inspections.

Immelt calls it "the next productivity revolution."

Predix came out of GE Digital, the $6 billion unit GE created to pursue its ambitions. Starting with the exact benefits customers were looking for, GE knew it had to move quickly into the digital space. They worked backward from there. More specifically, they needed a leader to spearhead the creation of a digital platform that would enhance industrial customers' productivity, a person who truly understood the business, could attract talent in Silicon Valley, who understood the potential and was entrepreneurial and could build a team.

GE found that person in Bill Ruh, who is now the chief executive officer for GE Digital, as well as being the senior vice president and chief digital officer (CDO) for GE. GE hired him from Cisco in 2011 to establish its Industrial Internet strategy and to lead the convergence of the physical and digital worlds within GE globally.

Specialized skills like Ruh's are one thing. But you need natural talent as well. Natural talent in employees is observable, if you take the time to look. It's a matter of noticing which tasks come naturally to the person, the ones that energize him and others around him.

If you're in sales, you may well have seen the person with the highest sales numbers get promoted to sales manager—and totally flop. If his bosses had observed him closely, they might have seen he's an *individual* contributor. He thrives on getting the deal done. That's what excites and drives him. He simply may not have the natural ability or desire to recruit other people and coach them to become superb salespeople themselves. If he can't motivate others and expand their capacity, he won't be successful in getting them to achieve the business priority of increasing sales. Such a person can make a fantastic salesperson but a lousy sales manager.

You want to also consider the mindset of the other person. Does he or she have an inner drive to succeed? Is the person open to change?

Let me make it more specific. For example, you want to know the mindset of a plant manager. If he's used to two inventory turns a month and you tell him you're going to thirty turns, how will he react?

We've all seen people who agree in meetings that something has to change and that they must do things differently, and then go out the door and do the same old thing. If you have people like that on your staff, what happens to the company's ability to execute?

When a person has worked at a company for a long time, the assumption is that the experience gives her great command over what's required. Yet over time the demands of the job may have changed. You have to ask whether this person has the ability to keep up with what is going on at the present time. Is she too rooted in doing things the way they've always been done?

If we go back to Walmart, you can see that situation today. The company mastered brick-and-mortar retailing, but the world is increasingly shopping online. Walmart needs people who have the ability to help close the gap with Amazon and maybe even allow the company to overtake the Internet giant.

Without the right people in the right jobs, a company cannot grow and thrive. In 1978, I was asked to advise on business strategy for a company that was doing $200 million in sales. The company was Intel, founded by three people we now call geniuses: Andy Grove, Gordon Moore, and Bob Noyce. These men had incredible energy, the ability to think outside the box—before that phrase had become a cliché—and the passion to create something that would permanently alter the world and produce results for shareholders and employees.

The secret of CEO Andy Grove, who managed the organization, was putting the right people in the right jobs. One day I was sitting in his office when he got a call from an engineer working at a company twenty times Intel's size. He said he would take a pay cut to work for Intel because he, too, wanted to do something new and exciting. The engineer was hired. His aptitude, attitude, and drive matched the job and the needs of the company. Without people who fit, Intel could not have become the giant it is today, with sales of more than $56 billion and earnings upward of $15 billion.

This idea of revisiting the fit between the person and the job is exactly what's needed today in rapidly changing industries, such as financial services, where consumers are increasingly interacting with companies through their mobile devices.

Dealing with Mismatches

How many of the people around you are mismatched to their jobs? When the mismatch is huge, the person tends to feel insecure but may not know what to do about it. He may complain at work and drain other people's energy. The best business leaders recognize when a person's natural talents don't fit the job, and they have the confidence to take action.

Effectively and quickly dealing with mismatches gives you an edge in execution. Yet many businesspeople—including some prominent CEOs I've known—don't do this. Over the years I've asked many of them about the greatest mistake they've ever made in managing people. The most common answer? "Waiting too long" to remove a direct report who was not matched to the job.

EXECUTION IN A NUTSHELL

I wrote a bestselling book with Larry Bossidy, the retired CEO of Honeywell, on how to execute effectively. I am not going to reprise *Execution: The Discipline of Getting Things Done* here, but let me give you a quick primer on how to work efficiently.

1. Be totally clear on what you want to accomplish.

2. Break goals down into time segments ("We will have this done in a week; that in a month") and milestones ("We know we will be halfway there when we do X").

3. If you run into an obstacle, ask for help.

4. Constantly monitor progress, and follow through.

That last one may be the most difficult thing to do. Bright people hate following through. For one thing, they believe it is micromanaging. For another, they think it is somehow demeaning to their subordinates to check up on their work.

But you have to follow through to make sure that what you said is clear and that progress is being made.

As Intel got bigger, some people could not fill the expanding—and ever-evolving—jobs. Management took appropriate action. Perhaps the person was better matched to a job elsewhere in the company. Perhaps Intel was no longer the right place for him to progress. There was a certain amount of management-driven turnover at the fast-growing company. If the company's leaders had ignored those mismatches, chances are we would not have heard of Intel today.

Why do leaders so often avoid the mismatch issue? They want to avoid conflict. I see over and over how managers prepare for these conversations, and then the day comes and they back off. That's understandable, but wrong.

Avoiding conflict hurts the business—and hurts the mismatched employee. Employees often complain that they're not happy in their job and attribute it to their work environment. Sometimes that is the problem. But a mismatch between a person's natural talent and experience and the requirements of the job is often the real source of despair.

When an unhappy (mismatched) person is asked to leave, the person often is at first shocked or saddened. But when she finds another company where her talents fit, her personal energy and engagement come alive. It becomes rocket fuel to progress further.

I know of one person, let's call him Paul, who started out as a salesperson in a $5 billion global company. He soon demonstrated the talent to be a manager. He got promoted to sales manager and eventually to head of all company sales, and he flourished. He truly cared for people and was able to stretch and inspire them. Because of his success, Paul became director of operations for an entire country, not just its sales department. Again, he did a superb job. From there, he was promoted to head the company's operation in Europe.

His continued success caught the attention of the CEO. As time went on, the CEO had a need to fill. A key division that had grown rapidly through acquisitions was beginning to fail. The person who had put the deals together was unable to execute, and as losses mounted, he had to be removed. The CEO asked Paul to take over the failing division. Although the division was in an industry he knew nothing about, Paul accepted the challenge. The new job was clearly an opportunity to show whether he had what it took to run the company one day.

Paul dove in, but he struggled from the start. The division needed someone who understood finance, and Paul was a marketing and sales expert. Six months into the job, he was floundering. With little to show for his efforts, he planned to change some people and bring in consultants. After all, he was not a quitter.

Meanwhile, lack of success was attracting his bosses' attention, and his prospects to eventually become CEO of the entire company seemed to fade. His energy lagged. Sensing that his career was in jeopardy, Paul resigned and took a job as CEO of an online commerce company, an area he knew well, one that called on all his natural talents. The fit was right, and his confidence and energy soon returned. He told me afterward that he felt "liberated" because he had found a match for his talents.

Another executive of a $23 billion business was a maverick at heart. He made decisions quickly, and the people who reported to him loved him because he would fully back them until they showed they were not worthy of his trust. His peers and his bosses, however, found him insulting. It was clear to them that he felt he deserved to have his boss's job and eventually become CEO. It was clear to everyone that despite his abilities, he was not a good fit for the company. As his frustrations mounted, his bosses and peers found his behavior even more objectionable.

Finally, a headhunter placed him as the CEO of a start-up company, where his natural talents and inner drive fit perfectly. In less than three years, he built the company into one that was larger in market value than the one he had left. He is now a very high-profile CEO.

Coaching

People who do well in a job also need attention. A true leader expands such employees' capacity by helping them channel their talents and develop their abilities so they can advance to the next level. Expanding capacity may mean giving them a "stretch assignment" that will help them to develop a new skill or gain a new perspective.

How would you feel if someone gave you positive feedback on the things you are doing well, while offering specific suggestions for developing your skills? Chances are you would feel you had a boss who cared for you, someone who wanted to help you improve and succeed. You would feel energized.

ASK

Not every company has a mentoring or coaching program. If your workplace doesn't, ask that one be created. And if the answer is no, find someone—or a series of someones—older and more experienced than you to help you grow.

When you get the feedback, listen with your ego turned off. The people working with you want you to improve. Remember that.

Most people don't like to hear (constructive) criticism. But the smartest people learn from it and expand their capacity.

I can tell you from experience that it works. And people who do it for those who report to them expand their own capacity in the process.

I used to hear about a guy who ran a small plastics division in Massachusetts. Every Sunday morning he would call the people who reported to him to discuss something he had seen in the *New York Times* that morning. This leader was using those phone calls to stimulate his people intellectually and expand their horizons. After about five Sundays, everybody was picking up the *New York Times* and discussing what they had read. They were bonding and gaining a broader view of business. (That man, by the way, was a young Jack Welch early in his career at GE.)

Perhaps you think you give people feedback when you do their annual performance review. In reality, performance reviews are rarely used to develop people. Most of the time they're simply a way to communicate a salary change based on last year's performance, or they're used to justify a promotion (or to explain why someone is not being promoted or is actually being fired). That is *not* the way to help people grow and develop.

What is the right way? Building on the person's strengths with feedback that is honest and direct. No sugarcoating.

In fact, every encounter is an opportunity for coaching, and the sooner the better. One businessperson was on track to be CEO of a large company. He got raises every year, got the highest bonuses. Everyone said he was fantastic. He inspired people and always delivered on commitments. But when the board got to discussing this person, one of the directors said: "He takes the hill very well, but somebody has to tell him which hill to take."

The assessment underlying that one sentence eliminated the candidate's chances of becoming CEO. In the eyes of one of his evaluators, the person had a fatal flaw—the perceived inability to set strategy. While quite a few people had noticed that flaw before, this was the first time it had ever been mentioned, and by the time it was, it was too late. The board thought he did not have the requisite skill to lead the company. It would have been much better for the person to have had that feedback ten years earlier, when he had time to develop.

Sometimes an adverse situation creates the opportunity for coaching. Let me give you one more story about Jack Welch.

Welch, a master at coaching, turned a botched presentation into a learning experience. He was CEO of GE at the time and had invited a group of middle managers to talk about the company's e-commerce strategy at the very beginning of the dot-com era. As one of them started to make his presentation, the equipment failed. There he stood in front of a very demanding CEO and ten of his peers.

What do you think the CEO did? Welch immediately sat back in his chair, looked at the group, and said, "Let's discuss what you would do if this happened in front of a customer." Welch knew that the person had rehearsed and prepared, and that this could have happened to anyone. Rather than admonishing the executive for not double-checking the equipment, which would have created a negative situation, he became a teacher and a coach.

Self-confident, secure leaders know that growing people is their responsibility. They love to give true feedback. By "true feedback" I mean saying what they really think. Too often people hesitate because they worry they may be wrong or they fear reprisal. But chances are your instincts are correct and the people you are trying to help by providing true feedback will improve over time. Some people admit that this kind of coaching is a good idea but say their company doesn't have the kind of culture that would support it. (See the box "Ask.") If that is the case where you work, you can still start to do it with three or four people who you believe would be receptive.

In one global company that did not have a policy of coaching people, I saw a young manager from Uruguay sit down with people one by one and make suggestions that would help them get better. In the culture he was from, it isn't easy to receive feedback. People see it as criticism. But he worked at it. You should see how grateful people felt toward this man. He turned his part of the company around in six months, and his performance was so good that within a year he was identified as someone who should be watched and given new leadership opportunities. He may become a CEO someday.

Coaching on the Business Side

Too often when leaders try to coach others, they focus only on behavior. Could the other person be less abrupt? Could he listen better? Asking those kinds of questions is good. But don't forget the business side. Can the person cut through complexity? Is the person selecting the right priorities? Is he specific? Does he execute?

Below I've included a letter you should read. It's a disguised version of a real letter, written by a CEO (let's call him Bob) of a $10 billion company to a division head (whom we'll call Tom). The company is number one in the United States and worldwide and has a good return on capital. It's a good business. Tom's division is probably in the top quarter of all competitors. Bob wrote the letter after meeting with Tom to go over his budget request.

July 31, 2015

Dear Tom:

Some thoughts about your budget proposal.

Your plan has to deal with lower sales and lower prices. Please get the team ahead of the curve. Don't pass up any orders. Your division is in the midst of a fundamental change, not a cyclical one; the organization will want to make it appear temporary. Don't let them. It isn't.

Let's allocate resources to growth markets. We talk about the future, but then allocate based on history. That needs to change.

Speaking of change, the European division needs radical change; the old guard is still in place. How can we get it oriented to company goals, not regional fiefdoms? Let's drop the old national name and integrate it into the total business.

Your primary product line needs energy and fire. It has to be operated more like your newer line—product by product, leader by leader, driving the new products. It is too complex; let's simplify it. It is a tough challenge.

Tom, 2016 will be your toughest year. I'm glad you're here.

—Bob

What do you see in the substance of the letter? What does Bob think Tom is missing? He thinks Tom is not seeing the change taking place in the business. That change is not a passing trend but a fundamental, structural shift in the business. What happens if Bob doesn't get Tom to focus on this change? How does it reflect on Bob's value as a CEO?

There's a second thing Bob questions. He's wondering whether Tom is devoting sufficient resources to the future. He wants Tom to look forward, not back. Bob is not just giving the guy a pat on the back and saying "nice job" or complementing him on a solid past performance. He's being very specific about what needs to improve. And you can bet he's going to follow through.

Put yourself in Tom's shoes. You know Bob values you very highly. Would this letter give you pause? Make you determined to do even better? Or lead you to quit?

If you are on board with Bob's feedback, you could see it as a road map. It is a clear guide on how to develop in your career. If you disagreed, you'd have to go back to Bob and discuss it.

Now read the follow-up letter, sent six months later:

January 23, 2016

Dear Tom:

I enjoyed attending your session last week. I thought you exhibited real energy in the room.

2015 was a pretty good year for your division. Inventories, receivables, and working capital all showed modest improvement. But results in Europe continue to disappoint and obviously must be fixed in 2016. How can I help you?

As we look to '16, there are several things I believe you have to think about.

• *Global marketplace.* The potential for radical change here is great. Is your team ready to make the dramatic shift in cost structure?

• *Value products.* Do we have enough emphasis on value products? That is where our program dollars have to go—now.

• *Suppliers.* The supplier management initiative must permeate the entire organization and become a way of life. Be sure you are setting the bar high enough.

• *Developing countries.* Between India and China, there are 2 billion bodies and an enormous potential market for us. I hope we can get a plan together in the first quarter that is 100% devoted to growing these emerging markets.

Finally, Tom, operationally for '16, I would like you to think in terms of a total second act. The division is going through a massive transition. You must be consumed by the opportunities and the challenges you will face. You can provide great leadership; you must see the glass as half full rather than half empty.

Thanks for your help in making the supplier management initiative happen. It will make a real contribution to the total company in '16.

—Bob

Here in the follow-up, the CEO is talking about cost structure, product line, sales decline, and growth. Out of all the complexity, he is coming up with a short list of items to concentrate on. He's not talking in generalities. He's not using the word "strategy." He's being specific. Half a year has gone by and there hasn't been much progress. The boss is asking, "How can I help you?" In other words, he thinks help is needed.

Note that Bob's coaching in these letters is not about personal things—how Tom can interact with people and the like. It's focused on the business side: Tom's ability to face the fundamental realities and needs of the business. Bob is trying to help Tom develop his business skills and his judgment about people.

Such sharply focused coaching is a true gift to the individual receiving it. Maybe these letters are too harsh, too candid for your junior colleagues to receive. You can soften the language. But do the coaching on the business side. Identify just one thing about the individual where improvement would have a positive impact on the person and the company.

Coaching Behavior

Here's a specific example of the kind of coaching you can do on behavior. A bright, hardworking, dedicated, loyal individual somehow feels constrained—perhaps "intimidated" would be a better word—in a group. The person is highly respected, but under the pressure of group dynamics, she does not feel strong enough to disagree. The person agrees to do something, knowing full well she doesn't intend to do it, because she believes the group's decision to be wrong. One-on-one, the person is very open and honest and expresses herself clearly. But in the group setting, she doesn't have the courage to challenge others, and instead agrees to commitments she cannot or does not want to meet. Such people grin and nod, but as soon as the meeting is over, the agreement is broken. They simply do not follow through on what they said they will do.

This weakness is debilitating to the individual and the group. It causes decisions to have to be revisited and reworked, and slows progress. It may well prevent the group from achieving its business priorities.

It's the leader's job to identify this weakness, help the individual become aware of it, and coach the person on how to overcome it.

Consider this example from a CEO of a large technology company coaching one of his direct reports new to the industry. The CEO writes a letter full of compliments for the first two pages, before identifying areas for improvement:

It will be important for you to enhance your performance in the two following areas:

1. You should delve more deeply into operational details of your businesses. Whether it is service levels or capital expenditures, you must be completely versed in the inner workings of each business and hold managers strictly accountable for high achievement. While you came from outside the industry, you are a quick study. Having a stronger knowledge base will serve you better.

2. Sometimes you are too sympathetic to people and accept plans or performance from them that are, in fact, substandard. Raise your standards. Always keep your standards at or above what we must achieve to propel us forward as a global company of excellence.

The CEO is basically saying that the person is being too nice. His behavior is getting in the way of results. Maybe the person is unsure of himself because he's still learning the industry. Maybe it is something else. The reason doesn't matter. The CEO is telling him to take charge and hold people accountable. I know of a businessperson who was described as fabulous, brilliant, a visionary, very committed. But he was told by his CEO that he was "not tough enough" to cut his losses. What did he mean? Maybe the manager had a fear of admitting failure and was holding on too long to a business that was losing money, or maybe he was continuing to pour money into a failing project, or maybe he was not facing up to the fact that a key person he had hand-picked was not up to the job. It could be all three. (And, of course, if the senior executive is unsure, he should ask the CEO for clarification.) But it was clear that the CEO wanted him to be more decisive, sooner.

If the person who gets the feedback makes the correction, the manager—and the company—will perform better, producing an edge in execution.

9

SYNCHRONIZATION

Synchronization expands the organization's capacity.

Talking about individuals alone does not fully capture the reality of an organization. Just think about your own experience. What's missing after you discuss mastering the business fundamentals and making sure the right employee is in the right job?

The answer? All the stuff that connects people to one another and allows them to move in the same direction with a minimum of friction.

Unless you synchronize efforts and link them to your organization's business priorities, you won't have an edge in execution. Moneymaking won't happen.

A synchronized organization is like a championship rowing team—people working together in rhythm accomplishing more as a group than any one individual could do alone.

> Synchronization makes the whole or-
> ganization better. It leverages the re-
> sources that are already in place and
> allows you to move faster, something
> that is vitally important today.

For a shopkeeper whose family works with him, synchronization is not a big issue. His children may not have precisely
the talents the business needs, but they usually coordinate their
efforts quite naturally. Similarly, in a small organization, everyone knows everything that's going on. They overhear one another on the phone; they go to lunch; they talk during the day.
They automatically adjust to one another. If there's confusion,
they stop and figure it out together.

But as an organization grows, and you have dozens if not
hundreds or thousands of people working together, synchronization becomes a greater challenge.

It is easy to understand why. To divide responsibilities, companies put in place a formal organizational structure. The moment that structure is created, the social interactions change.
Often the information flow from one part of the organization to
another gets clogged or distorted. The bigger the company, the
harder it is for people to share information, come to agreement,
and adjust their priorities. Decision-making slows. The edge in
execution gets blunted.

An All-Too-Common Scenario

Let me give you an example of what I am talking about. If you work in a large company, does the following sound familiar?

You're sitting in the quarterly review as a colleague plows through a two-inch-thick proposal for a big investment in a new product. When he finishes, the room falls quiet. People look left, right, or down, waiting for someone else to open the discussion. No one wants to comment—at least not until the boss shows which way he's leaning.

Finally the CEO breaks the silence. He asks a few mildly skeptical questions to show he's done his due diligence. But it's obvious that he has made up his mind to back the project. Before long, the other attendees are chiming in dutifully, careful to keep their comments positive. It appears that everyone in the room supports the idea.

But appearances can be deceiving. The head of another division silently worries that the new product will take resources away from her operation. The vice president of manufacturing thinks the first-year sales forecasts are wildly optimistic and will leave him with a warehouse full of unsold goods. But everyone keeps their reservations to themselves, and the meeting breaks up.

Over the next few months, the project is slowly strangled to death during a series of strategy, budget, and operational reviews. It's not clear who's responsible for the killing, but it's evident that the true sentiment in the room that day was the opposite of the apparent consensus.

In my career as an adviser to large organizations and their leaders, I have witnessed many occasions, even at the highest

levels, when silent lies and a lack of closure lead to false decisions. They are "false" because they eventually get undone by
unspoken factors and inaction. This happens because the people charged with reaching and acting on a decision fail to engage
and connect. Intimidated by the group dynamics of hierarchy
and constrained by formality and lack of trust, they don't act
decisively—or at all. There is a lack of synchronization.

Lack of synchronization explains why so many small shopkeepers and vendors never expand. They do not know how to
create mechanisms that bring people together in a meaningful
way, one that increases their individual abilities and builds the
capacity of the total business.

A lack of synchronization can keep a large company from
moving forward effectively. Today, if you are not growing and
responding quickly to changing conditions, your company is in
serious danger of being left behind.

> **Some people just can't make up
> their minds. The same goes for some
> companies—and their performance suf-
> fers as a result.**

An edge in execution requires mechanisms that synchronize
individual contributors, what I call "social operating mechanisms." Social operating mechanisms are critical if you are to
gain an edge in execution.

Walmart's Social Operating Mechanism

This classic example of a social operating mechanism remains one of the best I have ever seen. Perhaps that isn't surprising. It was created by one of the greatest retailers who ever lived: Sam Walton.

Every Monday through Wednesday, some thirty regional managers went out to visit nine Walmart stores and six of their competitors' stores in a given market. They'd gather a basket of goods and compare the prices. Back when this was going on, in the early 1990s, Walmart's goal was to have prices that were at least 8 percent lower than what major competitors were charging in the area, and these visits were one way of finding out that they actually were.

But the regional managers were looking at more than price tags. They were observing the merchandise, how it was presented, what consumers were buying, what the stores looked like, what the ambiance was, what new practices competitors were using, and how employees were behaving.

Go back to the fundamentals. Remember our conversation about consumers—who they are and what they are buying. You assess this through competitive analysis, which for Walmart was going on constantly.

Notice how many layers of people there are at Walmart between the regional managers and the store level where the action is: zero. What is the value of zero information layers? Speed and quality. There is zero delay. Zero filters. Zero distortion. And what is happening to the honing of the senses? The skill improves with practice, and people at Walmart practiced a lot.

On Thursday mornings, Sam Walton conducted a four-hour

session with a group of some fifty managers. They included the regional managers who visited stores, buyers, logistics staff, and advertising people. Maybe it would come out in the Thursday morning meeting that the Pacific Northwest region needed an additional hundred thousand gross of sweaters on the shelves by Tuesday, and that those sweaters hadn't been moving in the Northeast because it hadn't been cold enough. The inventory got adjusted.

So you see what was going on: information was being exchanged and integrated, decisions were made, and every participant was getting a total picture of the business and a feel for the competition that were no more than one week old. People were acting on unfiltered information gathered directly from consumers and frontline employees. Walmart was then, and continues to be, a truly consumer-oriented company.

Sam Walton's social operating mechanism brought his priorities from the fifty-thousand-foot level to the ground level, where the synchronization had to take place. At the same time, accountability was built in. If someone wasn't readily participating in the discussion—perhaps because she was not prepared—it was visible to everyone there.

The point in telling this story is not to get you to copy Walmart's social operating mechanism. You must determine for yourself where information sharing or joint decision-making is critical and design social operating mechanisms that are right for your company.

Designing Your Own Social Operating Mechanisms

Think about how you synchronize and integrate your efforts with other people at work. Chances are you do much of it through meetings. But as a social operating mechanism, most meetings are weak. Oftentimes the wrong people attend, the dialogue is unproductive, there's no leadership, no decisions get made, and there's no follow-through.

Find a better way. Do the work on the business side first. Set the priorities. Then take the time to design a social operating mechanism, whether a conference call or a fifteen-minute gathering, that gets information flowing and the right people talking. Keep Walmart's social operating mechanism in mind as you design yours to make information transparent to all the participants simultaneously, with zero filters, and with routine frequency.

A well-designed meeting is a social operating mechanism, and so is something as simple as a letter or report from the CEO that opens the information flow and creates new behavior. At one company I worked with, the new CEO knew employees at one of his plants were skilled and well-meaning, yet the company hadn't been earning a profit from this unit. Rework and high costs were killing the business. In his first thirty days on the job, the CEO introduced a profit-sharing plan and made sure that everyone understood how it worked. Then he started issuing weekly reports on the three items that were the biggest money guzzlers: the number of employees, the amount of re-work, and the percentage of damaged goods.

One thirty-year veteran, the head of manufacturing, was shocked by the reports. He said: "I didn't know we weren't making money. I could cut costs in half if you'd let me." The employee explained his ideas, and they made sense. Four months later, the plant was profitable. The weekly reports gave everyone a common view of the business and helped channel the company's human energy toward the business priorities.

Designing social operating mechanisms is a leadership task, not one for the human resources department. Use your creativity and take it on as a personal challenge. Then pay attention to the nature of the dialogue that takes place within those mechanisms, using the guidelines in the box "The Essentials of Dialogue" on page 152.

Leading Through Dialogue

You've got the right people in the room or on the line. How do you get everyone on, as the cliché goes, the same page? With dialogue. Talking to one another honestly, with no hidden agendas like the ones we saw in the earlier example. Through these conversations, information can be shared, assumptions challenged, and disagreements brought to the surface.

What that means is that the quality of the dialogue determines how people gather and process information, how and whether they make decisions, and how they feel about one another and about the outcome of whatever trade-offs or decisions get made. Dialogue can lead to new ideas as people trigger one another's imagination and build on one another's comments, and it can speed decision-making, which is a competitive advantage.

Dialogue is the single most important factor underlying the productivity and growth of the knowledge worker. Indeed, the tone and content of dialogue shape people's behaviors and beliefs—that is, the corporate culture—faster and more permanently than any reward system, structural change, or vision statement I've seen.

So, how do you create the right kind of dialogue?

Practice by using each encounter with teammates and other employees as an opportunity to model the kind of open, honest, and decisive dialogue you want to take place. Say what's really on your mind, and solicit others to do the same by asking questions in a nonthreatening way. Asking someone to clarify their point, for example, will draw out their thinking. Be sure to listen, and not to make snap judgments about the quality of the comment. In doing so, you help set the tone for the entire organization, even if you are not in charge.

Consistently practiced in social operating mechanisms, this kind of honest, direct dialogue will establish clear lines of accountability for reaching and executing decisions. You can also use dialogue to give feedback, to recognize high achievers, to redirect the behaviors of those blocking the organization's progress, and to coach those who are struggling. Here's an example.

The head of a U.S. multinational's largest business unit was making a strategy presentation to the CEO and a few of his senior executives. Sounding confident, he laid out his strategy for taking his division from number three in Europe to number one. It was an ambitious plan that hinged on making rapid and sizable market-share gains in Germany, where the company's main competitor was based and was twice his division's size.

The CEO praised the unit head for the inspiring and visionary presentation, then initiated a dialogue to test whether the plan was realistic.

"Just how are you going to make these gains?" he wondered

aloud. "What other alternatives have you considered? What customers do you plan to acquire? How have you defined the customers' needs in new and unique ways?"

The unit manager hadn't thought that far ahead.

"I have a couple of more questions," the CEO said. "How many salespeople do you have?"

"Ten."

"How many does your main competitor have?"

"Fifty," came the sheepish reply.

The boss continued to press: "Who runs Germany for us? Wasn't he in another division up until about three months ago? How familiar is he with the market?"

Had the exchange stopped there, the CEO would have only humiliated and discouraged this unit head, and sent a message to the others in attendance that the risks of thinking big were unacceptably high. But the CEO wasn't interested in killing the strategy and demoralizing the team. Coaching through questioning, he wanted to inject some realism into the dialogue. Speaking bluntly but not angrily or unkindly, he told the unit manager that he would need more than bravado to take on the formidable German competitor on its home turf.

"Instead of making a frontal assault," the CEO said, "why not look for the competition's weak spots? Where are the gaps in your competitor's product line? Can you innovate something that can fill those gaps? What customers are the most likely buyers of such a product? Why not zero in on them? Instead of aiming for overall market-share gains, wouldn't it make more sense to try to resegment the market?"

Suddenly, what had appeared to be a dead end opened into new insights and a new way forward. The meeting ended with the manager promising to come back in ninety days with a more realistic alternative. To make sure that happened, the CEO followed up with a one-page, handwritten note summarizing the meeting, and proposed some dates three months out to continue the discussion. Even though his strategy proposal had been flatly rejected, the manager left the room feeling energized, challenged, and more sharply focused.

Think about what happened. Although it might not have been obvious at first, the CEO was not trying to assert his authority or diminish the executive. He simply wanted to ensure that competitive realities were not glossed over. He was challenging the proposed strategy not for personal reasons but for business ones. And he also wanted to coach those in attendance in both business acumen *and* the art of asking the right questions.

The dialogue affected people's attitudes and behavior in both subtle and not-so-subtle ways. They walked away knowing that they should look for opportunities in unconventional places—and be prepared to answer the inevitable tough questions. They also knew that the CEO was on their side. They became more convinced that growth was possible.

And something else happened: they began to adopt the CEO's approach.

When, for example, the head of the German unit met with his senior staff to brief them on the new approach to their market, the questions he asked his sales chief and product development head were pointed, precise, and aimed directly at putting the new strategy into action. He had adopted his boss's style of relating to others as well as his way of eliciting, sifting, and analyzing information—a style his boss learned from the CEO. The entire unit grew more determined and energized.

THE ESSENTIALS OF DIALOGUE

Execution improves when the dialogue in social operating mechanisms is marked by four characteristics: openness, candor, informality, and closure.

Openness means the outcome is not predetermined. There's an honest search for alternatives and new discoveries. Questions like "What are we missing?" draw people in and signal the leader's willingness to hear everyone. It creates a safe environment to consider new ideas, and rethink old ones.

Candor is slightly different. It's a willingness to speak the unspeakable, to expose unfulfilled commitments, to air the conflicts that undermine apparent consensus. Candor means that people express their real opinions, not what they think team players are supposed to say. Candor helps wipe out the silent lies and pocket vetoes that occur when people agree to things they have no intention of doing. It prevents unnecessary rework and revisiting of decisions that saps productivity.

Formality suppresses candor; *informality* encourages it. When presentations and comments are stiff and prepackaged, they signal that the whole meeting has been carefully scripted. Informality has the opposite effect. People feel more comfortable asking questions and reacting honestly. The spontaneity is energizing.

If informality loosens the atmosphere, *closure* imposes discipline. Closure means that at the end of the meeting, phone call, or one-on-one interaction, people know exactly what is expected. Closure produces decisiveness by assigning accountability and deadlines. Lack of closure, coupled with a lack of sanctions, is the primary reason for indecisiveness and inaction.

A robust social operating mechanism consistently exhibits these four characteristics.

PART IV

YOUR PERSONAL AGENDA

10

YOUR PART IN THE BIG PICTURE

Here's what you need to do now.

By now you should be fluent in the universal language of business, comfortable with using (and understanding) terms such as "cash," "inventory turns," "profitable growth," and "satisfying customers." No matter what your job, you should have a shopkeeper's view of your company's total business. You should also have an appreciation for how moneymaking is valued by the stock market (should your company be public) and by companies that might be interested in acquiring (or being acquired by) your organization.

You are probably reading this book because you want to be a business leader. How can you use what you have learned here to improve the business, keeping in mind customers, cash generation, return on invested capital, and growth? How can you get results by tapping every individual's intellectual energy?

Link your own priorities to the big picture. If you're in human resources, for example, you can help people break out of their silos, and coordinate efforts with people elsewhere in the company to help ensure that the company has the right people in the right jobs. As we have seen, having the wrong person in place can have a tremendously damaging effect on each one of the business fundamentals.

If you work in information technology, maybe you can create links with customers and suppliers so your company can collaborate more easily. An in-house attorney can help by keeping up to date with legislative changes globally and staying alert for new opportunities that might arise as a result. Those in finance can assist with many kinds of decisions—whether to add capacity, how to improve pricing for better margins, where best to deploy cash, and the like—by providing accurate and timely information. Finance can also be a partner in analyzing the most promising growth opportunities.

But I hope you are convinced by now that your professional excellence alone is not sufficient. Just like the street vendor, you need to think like a businessperson.

If you do, your perspective will expand beyond a functional or departmental view to one where you see the total business. Your thinking will probably become more creative as a result. You will feel empowered to ask questions in any meeting, without fear of hierarchy or embarrassment. Ask the leadership in your group to have discussions about the universal laws of business, the fundamental building blocks that we have talked about throughout.

Maybe you can break new ground by coming up with a novel idea that relates to the overall business. Maybe you can help by simply reframing an issue, bringing the underlying assumptions to the surface, and challenging them.

What does it mean to reframe an issue? Here's an example.

Say you work for a car company and there is a need to cut costs on next year's model. Put on your businessperson's hat and ask, "Are there features that customers don't care much about and that can be eliminated to reduce cost?" Conversely, you can ask what customer needs are not being met. If you can meet them, would that create value, allowing you to raise prices? If so, how would that affect volume and utilization of manufacturing capacity? You always want to look at things from different vantage points to try to broaden the range of moneymaking options.

Assess the Total Business

Every company faces challenges. Begin by making sure you understand the ones your organization faces.

- What were your company's sales during the last year?

- Are they growing, declining, or flat? What do you think about this growth picture?

- What is your company's gross margin? Is it growing, declining, or flat?

- How does your margin compare with competitors' margins?

- Do you know your company's inventory velocity?

- Do you know your company's accounts receivables?

- Who are your company's largest customers?

- What is your company's return on invested capital?

- Is your company's cash generation increasing or decreasing? Why is it going one way or the other?

- Is your company gaining or losing against the competition in terms of market share, profitability, and the like?

Step back and get a total picture of the business. Does your assessment match the view you're hearing from senior management? Are there questions you should ask, or suggestions you can make?

Cut Through Complexity

Now think about the broader context your company operates in. What are the external realities of your particular business? Make a list of all the things that could affect your company's moneymaking ability.

- Is there excess capacity in the industry?

- Is the industry consolidating?

- Do you face stiff price competition?

- Might your business be affected by currency fluctuations or changes in interest rates (up or down)?

- Are you facing new competitors?

- Where is innovation coming from?

- What is happening in e-commerce? How might that affect the company?

Chances are your list of external considerations will be long, the complexity great. Decide which factors you think are significant. Are some of them connected? Are there certain trends?

Don't expect this to come easily. It takes practice to cut through the complexity, and you may not have all the information you need. You may have to ask for it.

Before you read on, take the time to determine a couple of patterns or trends you think are important, and write them here:

1.

2.

3.

Provide Focus

As you cut through the complexity, you will get a clear fix on what is happening in the world. Then you must determine the three or four business priorities for your group, department, or business unit. How will they combine to enhance money-making?

Some of you may have the intellectual capacity to cut through complexity but you're indecisive or afraid of being wrong. You may be tempted to say, "Can't I wait until all the facts are in and the picture is sharper?" Here's the rub: you make a bet even when you don't make a bet! That is, by choosing not to do anything different, you are choosing the status quo. So by deciding not to decide, you have made a decision. You have decided to keep things as they are.

Have the courage and conviction to provide focus for your area. You have to decide what your department, division, or business unit must do and what it must stop doing. You have to determine the business priorities. You can't have too many, you can't keep changing them, and you have to communicate them explicitly and repeatedly. And those priorities have to be consistent and aligned with your company's goals.

If your business skills and understanding are good—and, of course, you will always be working to make them better—you'll understand why that particular combination of business priorities will make money.

> **Don't get swept up in grandiose visions of what you want to accomplish. You should be able to explain what you need to do in clear, simple terms, and you should be able to explain how it will improve moneymaking.**

Apply your common sense. And your business sense. You will be surprised how many good ideas you can generate. Write your business priorities here:

1.

2.

3.

Help People Expand and Synchronize

Consider the individuals who report to you and the others you interact with in your everyday work life. You don't have to be a top executive to develop other people's talents and match them to the job, or to design social operating mechanisms that make groups of people function better. Find ways to share unfiltered information simultaneously and to bring conflicts to the surface.

- Think about the match between the jobs and individuals you supervise: What are the two or three non-negotiable requirements of the job now and two years out? (You want to keep the focus this tight for two reasons. First, twenty-four months is a foreseeable time frame. After that, it is extremely difficult to predict what will happen. And second, if you move out beyond two years, you might be tempted to say that it is too far away to think about and so you will never take action.)

- What are the two to three things you would call the individual's natural talents and drive?

- What is the one major blind spot the person has that might prevent him or her from growing further?

- How can you help coach this person?

Then focus on a work group, team, or the organization as a whole and ask:

- What is the speed of decision-making? Yes, you want to move quickly, but your mother was right: haste does indeed make waste, if it shortcuts the exchange of information and ideas. A quick decision without the right information brought to bear is invariably wrong.

- What is the quality of the group's decisions? Does the group strive for 100 percent consensus or 80 percent agreement? If you are aiming for 100 percent consensus, you are always going to reduce the decision to the lowest common denominator, and there are two things wrong with that. First, it is going to take a very long time to achieve that consensus, and during that time a competitor could pass you by. Second, you will invariably end up with a watered-down decision. It is far better to get to 80 percent agreement and then convince the other 20 percent to come along.

- Do decisions stick, or are they often revisited and reworked?

- Do people find meetings constructive and energy-building, or destructive and energy-draining?

How to Be a Leader

If you want to be a leader in your organization, you need to concentrate on three areas: business focus, building the best team possible, and synchronization.

Be a leader of the business. With the command and urgency of a street vendor, pick the three items you, and those reporting to you, should focus on. Don't try to cover the waterfront, don't keep changing your mind, and don't back away from the challenge. Make the priorities known by repeating them often.

Be a leader of people. Go beyond the street vendor to build an organization that can execute the business priorities. Find the right people for the job and take personal responsibility for releasing their energy and developing their skills, building their business acumen along the way. When someone's aptitude or attitude gets in the way of execution, address the issue.

Synchronize the organization. Link people's efforts to the business priorities. Create social operating mechanisms that increase the information flow and coordinate people's work. Make the group more decisive. Build the team.

Start at the beginning. Return to your earliest experience in business, when you understood the nucleus of delivering newspapers, selling lemonade, babysitting, waiting tables, or whatever it was you did to make money. Expand on your business acumen by practicing it in more complex situations. Don't be afraid to make mistakes and learn from them. Make judgments that reflect business acumen—that is, street smarts—and share your knowledge.

Don't let this book become just an intellectual exercise. Before you close the cover, start thinking in concrete terms. Be prepared to answer this question: what are you going to do to help your company's moneymaking efforts in the next sixty to ninety days?

Let the excitement begin.

ACKNOWLEDGMENTS

This book truly belongs to my siblings and cousins, who practiced the universal laws of business without benefit of formal education, and to the many shopkeepers in villages in India and other countries, who exercise business acumen every day of their lives. The real learning came from watching them, along with observing some of the best CEOs in the world. I am grateful to Jack Welch, Larry Bossidy, Ivan Seidenberg, and many other accomplished leaders who allowed me to see firsthand how their business minds work. CEOs such as Tadashi Yanai in Japan and Ning Tang in China prove beyond doubt that the fundamentals of business transcend geographical bounds.

I owe special thanks to Jac Nasser, former chair of BHP Billiton, who encouraged me to write the first version of this book as a teaching device when he was CEO of Ford.

I am also grateful to two superb editors whose enthusiasm and skillful editorial support brought this book to fruition. John Mahaney, a former editor at Crown Business, encouraged me to write the first edition of this book some sixteen years ago and guided the development of its content. Roger Scholl, also at Crown, recognized that while the universal principles of business are timeless, changes in the business landscape warranted an updated edition. He was instrumental in shaping the current version.

Paul B. Brown used his reader-friendly writing skills to ensure that the ideas are easy to grasp. He deftly incorporated the new material, ensuring a seamless reading experience. Geri Willigan, my longtime associate who worked with me on the first edition, made editorial and substantive contributions to this version as well.

I also wish to extend my appreciation to Cynthia Burr and Jodi Engleson, the two people in my office who keep my work life on track so I can accomplish projects like this. I am grateful for their competence and courtesy on a daily basis.

Last, I am grateful to continuous learners and strivers everywhere, who constantly search to deepen their knowledge, improve their organizations, and make the world a better, more prosperous place for all.

INDEX

RAM CHARAN is the author or coauthor of four bestselling books—*Execution, Confronting Reality, The Attacker's Advantage,* and *The Leadership Pipeline*—and twenty others. His book *Boards That Deliver* is used as a reference by boards of directors around the world. Charan is also an award-winning teacher, formerly at Northwestern's Kellogg School of Management, Wharton, and GE's famous training center at Crotonville, New York. Charan began his business career in Australia after earning an engineering degree in India. He went on to earn master's and doctoral degrees at Harvard Business School, where he was later an instructor. He is a noted expert on business strategy, execution, leadership, corporate boards, and building a high-performance organization. He has worked with the CEOs of some of the world's most successful companies, including GE, 3G, Bank of America, Verizon, Coca-Cola, Pladis, 3M, Merck, Aditya Birla Group, Tata Group, Summit Corporation, and Hindalco. He is on five boards, in Brazil, China, India, and the United States.